Smart Investing for Busy People

Smart Investing for Busy People

The 5-Step Strategy for Building Your Wealth Wisely

Bill Moyes

VERNAL V PRESS

For information address Vernal Press.
205 Cheyenne Mountain Boulevard,
Colorado Springs, Colorado 80906.

ISBN 0-9707547-7-9

Edited by Barbara Ash
Cover Design by Paige Thomas
Photography by Melanie Tutt
Printed in the United States of America
by Woodburn Graphics, Inc.

For my three wonderful children and, indeed, for all the children of the world. At some point in their lives, may they learn the insights contained herein, and prosper.

"He who receives an idea from me, receives instruction himself without lessening mine; as he who lights his taper at mine, receives light without darkening me."

-Thomas Jefferson

Contents

Introduction

At lunch with a friend recently, the conversation turned to his efforts to make his investment money grow for a more comfortable retirement. He'd read a couple of books on investing and his comment was similar to one I've heard from people frequently: "I've read some of those books and thought they had some smart things to say, but I could never take much advantage of them because I've got a full-time job. I'm just too busy to do what they tell you."

It's true. If you've read Ben Graham's *The Intelligent Investor*, Graham and David Dodd's *Security Analysis*, or Phillip Fisher's *Common Stocks and Uncommon Profits*, you've been exposed to some of the best thinking available on equity investing. However, unless you could dedicate many hours every week to put their advice to work, - digging into the financial statements and studying various aspects of a myriad of companies - you probably didn't benefit from them greatly.

In addition to these texts designed principally for full-time money managers, a second general class of investment books is written more for "everyman." Perhaps the best known of these is *The Only Investment Guide You'll Ever Need* by Andrew Tobias. It is full of tidbits of wisdom, covering a wide range of personal financial issues. Unlike tomes such as *Security Analysis*, it is not academic in its tone; it's actually fun to read. It covers everything from how to save money renting a car to the ins and outs of zero coupon bonds, probate procedure and penny stocks to EE Savings bonds, TIPS (Treasury Inflation Protected Securities), Trust funds of all types, ETF's (Exchange on Traded Funds), etc. It is like an encyclopedia of all things financial. If you want to learn a little something about almost anything under the sun in personal money management, this type of book is just the ticket.

Smart Investing for Busy People is quite different from either of these types of books. First, it assumes that you're busy doing what you want to do and that you don't have an interest in stopping that to become a full-time investor. Second, it is not an encyclopedia; it is a dedicated plan – a plan that a busy person can put to work today to provide a lifetime of growing assets successfully and prudently.

Necessity

I developed this approach the way many things happen in nature: by necessity. Although my parents passed some extremely valuable things on to me, a financial inheritance was not one of them. I started coming into some money, however, "the old-fashioned way." I had founded and run a few companies with a long-time friend and business partner and we subsequently sold some of them. The businesses were a collection of radio stations and service companies that provided market research and consulting for media.

So the resulting "liquidity events" that the sales produced created the need to invest money wisely and safely, but I was in the same boat you may be in now. No one I fully trusted could tell me how to do this. I'd gotten an MBA from one of the better business schools and spent many years running businesses. But investing is different than running a company, and they don't teach what you'll learn from this book in most colleges or business schools. They should, but they don't. In fact, in many places of higher learning they teach some things that are counter to prudent investing. (I'll touch on a few examples later.)

Investment professionals that I knew were all too happy to sell me something, but there was no sensible holistic investment plan in their minds that they could spell out. And trusted friends – people not out to sell me anything - really didn't have a well-thought-out approach to money management either. In fact, the more I have spoken with people on the subject over the years, the more I realize that few people do. They may have some interesting insights, like pieces of a puzzle, but they don't have the complete picture…a comprehensive integrated approach to put money to work.

So, not having a particularly good financial strategy at that time, I invested the money with a couple of money managers and, through brokers of good repute, directly in some companies and mutual funds. I also purchased some real estate for investment purposes (i.e., in addition to the investment in my home.)

As time went on, the real estate investments did well, but I grew increasingly dissatisfied with the performance and the advice I was getting on the "stocks and bonds" side. You've probably discovered this already, but all the people who are anxious to help you with your investments – brokers, money managers, etc. - have an agenda. They all have one because they need to make money from the relationship. Some agendas are more subtle than others, but they all have potential conflicts of interest.

The worst conflict of interest seemed to be with the personal broker, especially in the days before commissions on trades had been broadly minimized due to the emergence of discount brokers. Forget for a moment that the stock picking ability of these people was not exactly on a par with Warren Buffett (the world's second richest person, due principally to his acumen in buying good companies at low prices.) The real problem was this: personal brokers were judged at their companies by the amount of profit generated from their clients. Profits were principally generated for the brokerage firm through transactions...the more transactions, the more commissions. So there was a conflict of interest such that what generated profits for the broker (lots of buying and selling of securities) generated lower returns for the investor. How did this happen? There were – and still are - three negative effects of frequent trading (i.e. high portfolio turnover):

1. The costs of the trades themselves in commission expense. These days, commissions don't amount to a lot, but they still count against returns.

2. The increased burden on long term returns that taxes cause in a high turnover portfolio. Let me give an example to make this clear. If you bought a portfolio of fine companies and held it for ten years without selling anything, you would incur no tax on any of the gains until you sold the stocks at the end of the ten years. All the gains in value achieved each year would grow without any diminution from taxes. But more turnover means more gain having to be realized along the way and more taxes eating away at monies that would otherwise be growing your wealth. In the long run, high turnover has a sizable negative effect on after-tax performance.

3. Perhaps the least appreciated but most pernicious effect: the tendency of the high-turnover portfolio not to take full advantage of the increasing profits, and attendant rising

value, of the high-quality companies one holds. In other words, high turnover leads to getting out of the winners way too early. You hear about people who regret having sold Microsoft or Wal-Mart prematurely. Here's a more recent example. I bought stock in the Chicago Mercantile Exchange (Ticker Symbol: CME), the world's largest futures exchange, back in 2003 at about $67. By the first half of 2004 it had gone to $100. At that time, many brokers undoubtedly encouraged their clients - clients who were similarly fortunate in buying the company around $67 - to take a gain on this investment by selling. If they took the advice, they made 49% in less than a year, not counting the tax bite on the gain. Hard to argue with that advice, right? Congratulations. Except that "The Merc", as it is called, went to $200 later in 2004, $300 in mid-2005, $400 in early 2006, and $500 in late 2006.

Money managers who charge a fixed fee (an annual charge based upon a percent of your assets under management with them) are not generally tempted by such foolishness, but I found myself disappointed by the results I was realizing for the fee being paid. And many managers –when all the types of fees are considered - don't charge a paltry 1% of your asset total yearly; they can and do charge considerably more. Furthermore, you pay such fees each and every year, even though the manager may be making suggestions that cause you to lag the market badly. In fact, you pay the fees even if you lose 10% or 20% of your money in a year - either due to a general market downturn ***or*** the manager's picks doing especially poorly. The idea of paying someone a lot of money in a year when one's portfolio loses value – maybe a lot of value - does not sit well with me. I have an unfortunate friend who paid sizable fees in 2001-2002 to the "High Net-worth Individuals" department of one of the big name firms, while his investments lost over $3 million in value. That just doesn't seem right.

Moreover, that idea of the manager being paid pretty much the same ***regardless of actual performance*** doesn't hit me as particularly sensible. Where, you have to ask, is their incentive to achieve the maximum return…to really knock it out of the park on your behalf? Sure, there's incentive not to lose the right to manage your money (and continue to earn those fees) if they do too poorly, but that is not exactly a rousing call to excellence, is it?

I had read about Warren Buffett's approach when he first started an investment partnership many years ago, and it seemed more sensible. When he had a good year (performing above a 6% return), he split the gain that year with his partners such that ***they*** got 75% of the upside and ***he*** got 25%. If he didn't grow the assets by at least 6%, he got nothing. Now that young man was motivated. And his results were phenomenal- almost 31% on average per year. Everyone was happy.

The idea of paying a modest base fee to a manager each year seems reasonable to me, because they have to cover their costs of doing business whether they have a good year or not. But I like the concept of seeing that they are very motivated to perform well on my behalf. I want the manager to get a big payday when I get a big payday.

After several years of performance disappointment and increasing concern about the conflicts of interest and lack of sensible motivation and reward, I embarked on a mission to discover everything I could about intelligent approaches to investing. I read everything I could get my hands on – books, essays, and articles by all kinds of respected investment professionals, I spoke to friends and business colleagues who I knew had been successful with various aspects of their investments, and I interviewed the investment professionals that these folks, in turn, said they had benefited from over the years.

What resulted from this effort was the development of a strategy that I and others have used with great success, primarily because it is based on principles that just make good sense. I think you'll get a clear view of that as you read.

The Approach

One principle that has always struck me as fundamental is that the most important thing about making money is not losing it. Of course, every financial adviser and fund manager would profess to agree with that. They may also profess to have a scheme to accomplish it. But when the markets get rough – really rough - most of those advisers, who claim to believe in the sanctity of your not losing money, post significant losses. And I'm not just talking about the small fish. One of the best known and most admired fund managers of our time is Bill Miller, manager of the only fund that has beaten the return of the S&P 500 for 14 years in a row. His Legg Mason Value Trust Fund (symbol: LMVTX) had assets under management as of December 31, 2006 of $21 billion. Beating the S&P for 14 years in a row is a tremendous record, really, since it's been estimated that about 75% of all mutual funds under-perform the S&P 500 each year. But in 2002, when the S&P 500 went down 22.1%, the Legg Mason Value Trust beat it by "only" being down 18.8%. Ouch.

Certainly Miller is brilliant and since 2002 he has come back, almost reaching the peaks the fund achieved in 1999 and 2000, but that's still a big loss. It can take a long time to regain losses so that they are not permanent capital losses. Think about this for a moment. If the value of your portfolio falls 50%, you have to come up 100% to just break even. And many funds and portfolios fell 50% ***or more*** over that 2000-2002 period. Doing all you can to be safe and minimize your downside just makes good sense.

So the steps of this investment system are designed to integrate safety – the avoidance of long-term capital loss - first and foremost. And the steps are meant to be sequential. You cannot really invest in high return opportunities safely unless you first take some basic steps.

As you read, if you find you've already accomplished certain of the early steps of the approach, that's fine. You can comfortably move on. Just be sure your personal financial situation doesn't skip any steps.

Promises About This Book

1. **It's written in Plain English.** If you've read books on investing in the past, you know that the authors can occasionally lapse into rather arcane financial language or concepts. I've tried to avoid using any fancy lingo from the financial elite or any confusing academic formulae.

   While the subject matter of the book is not, as a friend of mine jokes, "rocket surgery", there are a few notions that may not be intuitively obvious at first. I'd like this book to be accessible to both experienced business mavens ***and*** those with limited knowledge of personal finance, so I'll take time to explain these slightly more challenging concepts in a way that will hopefully be clear for all. Sensible things, if they truly are sensible, can be explained simply.

2. **It's to the point.** Don't you resent business and self-improvement books that go on and on (padded with unhelpful meanderings) to fill 300 or more pages when their ideas could have been conveyed effectively in far less space? That alone is a good reason to keep it short. Moreover, this book is not lengthy because it's written "For Busy People."

3. **It's focused.** There are endless financial instruments and investment concepts that could be discussed and each has intricacies that we could cover. But I have focused just on the financial assets and concepts that a busy person needs and can deal with. I stay away from those which are too risky, in my opinion, to be worth the potential rewards (e.g., commodities trading, penny stocks), those which would require too much of your time and perhaps some specialized expertise to do correctly (such as managing a portfolio of apartment buildings or trading futures and most options), and those which I don't feel are attractive if you are aiming to maximize long-term wealth building while avoiding dire consequences in a serious market downturn (e.g., index funds.)

4. **Its message is timeless.** To illustrate concepts, a number of facts cited and examples used are specific to a certain time frame or date. But the ***principles*** that empower this investment approach are timeless.

PREPARING YOURSELF TO INVEST CORRECTLY

Chapter 1

The Basics

As I mentioned in the Introduction, the things you will read about in this chapter, as well as the steps of the strategy contained herein, deal with issues that are important, but basic. If, as you read through the chapter, you find that you are fully conversant in these matters and that your personal investing program already incorporates these steps, feel free to move right to Chapter Two.

Lessons of the Power of Compounding

In my yearly talk to the investment club at a local high school, I always find myself wishing I were a teenager again. This is not to relive the joys of adolescence, but to take full advantage of the immense opportunity kids have through the power of compounding over a very long time period. Most of them have no idea of that power. They can have zero assets to begin with; they still have the power.

How can a teen with little or no money do any investing? Well, consider a couple of things. Let's imagine for a moment that you are a teenager...a reasonably intelligent teenager. What else do you have going for you?

First, for a while you will most likely be able to rely on your parents to take care of your living expenses, so any money that you do acquire ***could*** be put into prudent investments if you chose.

Second, for the next few years – maybe through college - you will have the ability to earn money doing chores, summer jobs, part-time jobs while in school, etc. while having that low cost of living. You could also explain to your folks and relatives who normally give you "stuff" at holidays, your birthday, graduation, etc., that you are focused on learning all you can about investing and that if they ever feel inclined to give a gift, you'd really appreciate that gift being a little cash that you could add to your small investment portfolio.

Third, because you are so young, you can let whatever investments you have grow and grow for a very long period of time. To make the math easy, if you invested, say, $1,000 per year in the stocks of good companies from ages 15 - 21 (seven years), and you were fortunate enough to have those investments grow at 15% per year after tax, what kind of money do you think that would amount to at age 55?

Before answering that, let's address a question that may have popped into your mind. 15% per year return...isn't that high? It's true that 15% is a somewhat higher return or growth rate than what the general ***market*** has achieved over the very long term (which is more like 10.5%), but consider:

1. Quite a few investors and funds have achieved better than 15% returns over the long term using the investment principles upon which this book is based, and ...

2. If all you want to do is match the return of the market, that's easy. Just buy an index fund. Anybody could tell you that. If you buy the Vanguard Index 500, for example, you will mimic the S&P 500 return, less a small annual fee. When the S&P 500 goes up 10%, you will go up almost 10%. And when the S&P falls 22.1%, as it did in 2002, you will go down about 22.1%. My goal, however, is to teach you how to have a reasonable chance of doing considerably better than the market and to set up your financial assets so that your investment success will not be dictated by – or terribly affected long-term by - the whims of the general market.

So, bear with me on the 15% return rate for the time being. Back to the question: What would the collective investments made by the teenager from ages 15-21 be worth at age 55?

What's at work for you here is the power of compounding - one of the most important principles of investing. The first year, that $1000 you invest grows 15%, and your gain is $150, of course. During the second year, if the money grows at the same rate, you wind up ***not*** with $150 gain, but 15% of $1150 ($1000 original investment plus the $150 you earned during the first year), so that you end the second year with $1,150 plus $172.50, or $1322.50.

At a 15% compounding rate, money roughly doubles every 5 years. It's a beautiful thing. Witness:

Start:	$1000.	
End of Year 1:	$1150.	($1000 plus $150, 1st year return)
End of Year 2:	$1322.50	($1150 plus $172.50, 2nd year return)
End of Year 3:	$1520.85	($1322.50 plus $198.37, 3rd year return)
End of Year 4:	$1748.89	($1520.85 plus $228.13, 4th year return)
End of Year 5:	$2011.24	($1748.89 plus $262.35, 5th year return)

The bottom line is that by age 55, the aggregated value of seven $1000 investments made between ages 15-21 would be worth approximately $1,232,000!

Because of this power of compounding, it makes sense to start investing as soon as you can in your life and to let the wealth grow for as long as possible.

Consider that last idea for a minute. If, in our hypothetical example above, you got to age 50 (instead of 55) and decided to take out your accumulated investments and spend them on something, you'd have one-half of $1,232,000, or $616,000. What a difference five years makes when compounding is at work! And, looking at the other side of that coin, if you got to age 55 without touching the funds and decided to keep them invested just ten more years until retirement at age 65, they would grow to almost $5,000,000, assuming the same 15% average annual growth rate.

Now, as I said, a 15% average after-tax rate of return over the long term may seem overly-optimistic to you, since it is higher than the market's long-term history by about five percentage points and taxes can put a drag on after-tax returns. But consider a couple of things.

At the moment, tax law allows a teenager, starting at about age 10 or 11 (whenever they can reasonably be expected to have "earned income,") to set up a Roth IRA where he or she can add not $1,000, but up to ***$4,000*** per year to put into investments. That earned income can result from parents giving them a yearly check for helping with things through the year, for example. And, in this IRA they can invest without being subject to paying yearly taxes on the investments. The maximum amount by which a Roth IRA for minors can be funded tends to grow as time goes by, so the amount may be greater than $4,000 by the time you read this. And teens don't have to stop funding their Roth IRA at age 21; they can do it throughout their life if they want to. Not only will they not pay taxes on the gains from year to year, but, if they wait to take the money out until age 59, they won't pay any taxes at all, even when it's all cashed in. And there are even certain circumstances wherein monies can be taken out before age 59, tax-free.

Moreover, as I mentioned, using the investment principles we will discuss in this book, many individuals and funds have accomplished a 15% return or better over a long span of years. The most notable example of flying past the market's performance is the years of the Buffett Partnership, Ltd. (1957 to 1969, when Buffett was picking companies to invest in, as opposed to swallowing companies whole as in the later Berkshire Hathaway days.) He managed to turn in a 30.4% average annual compounded rate of return over that period. This super performance was ***not*** achieved when the market had a long hot streak. In fact, the market during those 13 years had an average annual growth rate of only about 8.4%, a bit short of its long term 10.5% history. The partnership's amazing performance was due primarily, I believe, to two things: (a.) the smart principles of value investing and (b.) a motivated, bright fellow, in Buffett, who did a particularly good job of practicing them.

In any case, a good result is certainly not impossible for you as our hypothetical teenager. And, even if you fail to become a millionaire based upon that $7,000 of initial investment, think of how much you would learn about investing smartly to guide you in the many subsequent years of life when you will undoubtedly have considerably greater sums to invest.

Personal Debt

If you want to invest smartly, you first need to "get your house in order" a bit. If you plunge right into acquiring financial assets – even good ones - without taking the steps outlined in this and the next few chapters, you are not preparing yourself to do well safely, and you may be putting yourself squarely in harm's way.

The first step in the process is to rid yourself of virtually all personal debt. There is ***one*** – and only one - kind of debt which, in the right circumstance, is smart debt to carry and that is a mortgage on your home (and, perhaps, a vacation home). However, even that type of debt only makes sense if certain things are in place, which will be covered in detail in Chapter 3. All other debt should go, most especially, of course, any credit card debt.

OK, I'll bet you know all about the evils of carrying a balance on a credit card, but that doesn't mean it's not happening right under your nose. Bear with me as we take a moment to discuss it.

First, I'm not suggesting that anyone cut up and throw away their credit cards. They are a wonderful convenience. I carry very little cash and charge everything I possibly can on plastic. But I also pay off my credit card bill well before the due date every month, so I never pay any "finance charge" (the euphemistic term for the onerous, if not usurious, interest that credit card companies charge on any balance you do not pay off immediately). The only time you'd want to destroy your credit card – or, more likely, that of someone else in your household – is if you couldn't be sure that the balance on the card was going to be paid in full every month.

The credit card I normally use has an interest rate charge on outstanding balances that varies from day to day. Today that rate is 18.49% per year. The rate on "cash" on this credit card at the moment is 23.99% per year. "Cash," in this context, is either a cash advance through an ATM machine or a check you write yourself so that you can borrow money on the credit card. Those are the checks that the credit card companies are thoughtful enough to include in your billing envelope each month.

Clearly, there are credit cards with lower rates than 18.49%, but they are still pretty expensive. I never cared about securing a lower interest rate credit card because, of course, I never pay interest at all. The balance always gets paid within the grace period. Like many folks, I use this particular card all I can in lieu of cash because it gives mileage credit on my favorite airline.

Now, why would anyone pay credit card-related finance charges? Let's consider. There are two reasons people might borrow from a credit card by not paying off the balance totally each month.

The first case is when someone simply does not have enough money to pay off the card. That's a sad situation, but this book is ostensibly being read by people who are not destitute. You, as a reader, are someone with money to invest, so this reason for not paying off the card totally probably does not apply to you.

In the second and more common situation, you have the savings or income stream to pay your credit card fully each month, but figure you can afford the finance charge, so you don't pay it off - you let it ride. Let's analyze the consequences of this decision. Say you have $50,000 in a money market account earning 4% interest, yet you're carrying $20,000 in credit card debt. By forgoing paying off the credit card fully, you are paying, perhaps, 18% on the $20,000 card balance, while only earning 4% in your money market account. So on that $20,000 you have a net ***negative*** investment of 14%. How does that make any sense?

Now, although you may be content knowing that ***you*** would never fail to pay off your credit card within the grace period, it could still easily be happening in your household. If you have credit cards for your spouse or an adolescent son or daughter, have you looked at their credit card statement lately? If ***they*** get the bill each month, you may never see it. There may be balances being carried without your knowledge. Trust me: this happens. It happened to me and I was totally unaware of it.

If you do discover that you have some credit card debt at the moment, let's think about that debt and your wisest investment choices. Let's imagine that you have a balance of $20,000 on a card, that the company charges 18% interest, and that you have exactly $20,000 you'd like to invest. Great! Pay off your credit card and keep it at zero…that's the very best investment of your money. Where else are you going to earn an average annual compounded rate of return of 18% safely and with absolute surety? By this I mean that you can be 100% assured that as long as you carry that $20,000 in credit card debt, you will be paying 18% (or some other odious rate). Sadly, I cannot tell you a place where you can safely put to work the $20,000 you have at anything close to a ***guaranteed*** 18% return each and every year. And, if I could, you'd just be breaking even! If you pay off that card, it's 100% as good as investing with an 18% return because you've been able to forego having to pay the (absolutely assured charge of) 18%...maybe more.

Now, if all you have to "invest" is the amount needed to pay off your debts of this sort, that's fine. That's a great investment and you can stop right there and feel good. It's not everyone who can find guaranteed 18% investments. And you can consider other alternatives – things that can actually build wealth – when you accumulate more money to invest.

If you have more to invest after paying off the debt, read on.

Car Loans, Etc.

You may be tempted to hang on to some other types of personal debts, such as an auto loan, because the interest rate is a lot lower than 18%. Is that wise? Auto loans today charge an effective annual interest rate in the neighborhood of 7% and the interest you pay on an auto loan is not tax-deductible. So the cost to you is the whole 7% per year - the IRS is not helping you defray any interest expense as they do with most mortgages. The operative question is this: if you take on (or keep) the auto loan and dutifully take the amount of money you would have spent to buy the car to put into an investment, is there a good chance you'll earn more than 7% per year (after taxes) with that investment over the length of the auto loan? If you felt very sure about beating 7% after tax, it might be a smart loan to take, but can you feel sure about beating 7%?

An auto loan is generally a short-term loan (as opposed to a 30-year fixed rate mortgage.) For this example, let's say it's a 5-year loan. What has happened to the equity markets over the past five years in terms of average annual compounded rate of return? In the five years ended December 31, 2006 the S&P returned 6.18% average return per year (including not only the rise in stock prices in the index, but also the dividends one would have received by owning those stocks, reinvested). That's 6.18% ***before*** taxes.

Can you be highly confident of beating the interest rate of an auto loan with investments over the next five years? You may very well do it over the long term if you follow the tenets of this book, but ***in any five year period*** it's not a sure thing. And having to pay the 7% for the auto loan is a sure thing. Why take the chance?

So...

Smart Investing Step One:

Pay off *all* your personal debts, with the *possible* exception of a mortgage.

We'll discuss when a mortgage makes sense in Chapter 3. I'm not trying to be a tease. You have to understand the concept in Chapter 2 before you can judge whether having a mortgage makes sense in your particular case.

Living Below Your Means

Here's a simple fact: the more it costs you to live, the less of your money you can put to work growing your wealth.

This begs a couple of personal questions. How old are you? Considering your age and general state of health, how long might you live? If you are very near your full life expectancy (especially if you are not in good health), the idea of putting money toward growing your wealth, apart from leaving enough for a spouse to get along, may not matter alot. Have a great time! Put down this book and go do something you enjoy!

On the other hand, if you are likely to live quite a lot longer, then you have to consider the only disconcerting part of that prospect: the possibility of running out of money or being forced to work when you are 75 or 80. That, primarily, is why most people invest - it's not so much to get rich, but to have plenty to be comfortable and have those we love be comfortable.

In *The Millionaire Next Door*, authors Thomas Stanley and William Danko, after conducting extensive research with over one thousand millionaires, cite the most common qualities that millionaires possess, suggesting a causal relationship to their amassed wealth. At the top of their list: ***frugality***. The authors came to this understanding after asking the millionaires 249 questions about their behavior and attitudes, so it was very comprehensive in its scope.

Theirs is a study of those who have built wealth, not necessarily those with a big income or those who attain high social status or live in palatial homes. As they note, "Wealth is what you accumulate, not what you spend."

Warren Buffett is a wonderful example of this kind of frugality and eschewing of the high life. The most successful investor of all time, worth some 36 billion dollars, lives in Omaha, Nebraska – in what sort of house? I've driven by it, just out of curiosity. It is a nice comfortable-looking house of around 6,000 square feet with attractive, but not opulent, landscaping. Records show that in 1958 he paid $31,500 for it and it's supposedly worth about $700,000 today. Buffett is an example to us all not only in how he makes money, which we'll discuss, but also how he spends it (or doesn't over-spend it.) OK, he did buy a second home in California and a corporate jet which he sheepishly calls the "Indefensible," because he recognizes the somewhat unwarranted nature of such an extravagance. But, let's face it, for a guy worth as much as Warren, these are little treats. Everything is relative. He's still a very frugal man.

Conversely, let's look at what a lack of frugality can cost you. I had a friend who bought a Rolex watch about 20 years ago and boasted a bit about it. I think it cost him about $10,000 at the time. Now, let's say that instead of buying that Rolex, he'd put that $10,000 into Buffett's Berkshire Hathaway stock, which was selling in early 1987 at around $3,300 per share (For a "A" class share, not the lower-cost "B" shares) so he'd have been able to buy about 3 shares. Three shares sounds like an insignificant amount, doesn't it?

But if he had ponied up for the three shares and just let them sit there and appreciate, they would be worth about $106,000 ***per share*** today, totaling $318,000. What do you suppose that 20-year-old Rolex is worth now?

If you pick up a copy of The Robb Report or similar magazines, you are inundated with ads for all kinds of incredibly expensive watches, jewelry, yachts, leather goods, super-luxury cars…not to mention an $8,000 bottle of cognac! Even if you don't partake in the more "ultra" of these possessions, you may indulge yourself at some level, even if you just drive a high-end car.

In accounting terms, homes, cars, boats, etc., are officially classified as "assets". You list them on your statement of net worth, right along with cash and savings, bonds, stocks, investment real estate, private businesses, etc., on the assets side of the ledger. But there is a big difference between homes, cars, and boats on the one hand and private businesses, stocks and bonds on the other. How much money does your car make you each year? How much cash does your residence throw off each year?

You have to admit it: they don't make you money. They actually ***cost*** you money. In the case of homes – especially big, fancy homes with beautiful grounds – the yearly maintenance costs can be tremendous. So, although your residence, boats, and cars are "assets", they are clearly not the same kind of assets that investments in good companies or other real estate are. I think of them as "negative assets" because the higher their price, the more negative their effect on one's wealth and wealth-building capabilities.

Now, you may argue that homes (unlike cars, for example) could be considered "positive assets," because good homes appreciate in value. And there's no doubt that good homes, if bought correctly, almost always appreciate over the long term. But will you ever benefit from that price appreciation? If you live in that beautiful house until you die, you will not benefit from its increase in value (your heirs will, but not you). Ah, you say, you'll sell it and realize the appreciation. Good! One of the nice things about a home as an investment is that the government allows you to keep the first $500,000 of gain on a home tax-free. Downsizing, particularly when you no longer need 6000+ square feet because the kids have grown up and moved out, is commendable.

But what are you going to live in when you sell the house? If the answer is a house in another place, the realization of wealth gain will be limited to the difference between the values of the old home and the new home (less any taxes on the gain over $500,000, of course.) In any case, you still have to live somewhere. Your residence, especially when you consider its maintenance costs and lack of ability to create income, cannot really be considered a ***wholly*** "positive asset."

Expensive cars, boats, planes, etc. almost always depreciate in value and are clearly "negative assets" in that they cost you money initially and on an ongoing basis, sapping funds you could otherwise put toward acquiring "positive assets" and, thus, growing your wealth.

What's so good about acquiring "***positive*** assets" (assets that actually make you money and grow your wealth, acquired through investing)? In a nutshell, when the income from your positive assets is equal to or greater than your cost of living, you have realized total financial freedom. You are free to work or not work. If you're not ready to "kick back", you can choose exactly what you want to do for work, including volunteering at some worthy non-profit organization that gives you great psychic income, but pays little or nothing. You don't have to worry about running out of money or being forced to work when you're older if you choose not to.

In fact, you can achieve financial freedom even if the yearly cash flow from your investments is less than your cost of living. You can simply harvest part of the gain in value each year from equities you own to cover the shortfall. We'll discuss this more full in future chapters, but to clarify the point for the time being, let's imagine that your cost of living is $100,000 per year (just to make the math easy.)

One way to cover your living needs is to own bonds and live on their interest each year. Let's say you wanted to have enough in U.S. Treasuries to produce ***all*** of your $100,000 per year in living needs. Since Treasury Notes (2- to 10- year maturities) currently pay in the neighborhood of 4.5% interest each year, it would take something on the order of $ 3.1 million worth of treasuries to throw off $100,000 post-tax. Treasuries are exempt from state tax, but not federal tax, so, assuming a 28% federal tax bracket, you need a pre-tax annual yield of about $139,000 to get $100,000 post-tax, which means you need about $3.1 million in treasuries paying 4.5% interest (4.5% of $3.1 million equals about $139,000.) That's a whole lot of money in bonds, earning little each year.

But if you had a lesser amount – say, $2 million - invested in the stocks of great businesses (instead of treasuries), then, over the long term, the stock values will rise from year to year, usually at a much greater rate than bonds. This is true even if none of the stocks in your portfolio are companies that give a current dividend (i.e., don't yield what is normally thought of as income). So you could harvest (i.e. sell) $100,000 in stock value each year (after tax), and live on that, letting the rest accumulate to grow the total value of your portfolio. Of course, the growth in the value of your equities, unlike income from treasuries, will differ from year to year. Some years might be flat (no growth) or worse, while some might yield 20% or more. So you would just harvest more in the "fat" years and less in the "lean."

These scenarios show that there is more than one route to financial freedom, as long as your investments are large enough. That's the key: getting to where you have enough in "positive assets."

It's clear, therefore, that judiciously reviewing your various costs of living and cutting back where you can – doing all you can to avoid the temptations of living expensively - has two critical benefits:

1. It allows you to free up more of your income on an on-going basis to invest in wealth-producing assets.

2. You achieve financial freedom more quickly because the difference between your cost of living and your income from wealth producing assets is lowered, or even eliminated.

So...

Smart Investing Step Two:

Reduce your cost of living as much as possible so that you continue to grow your "positive assets" – your investments – as aggressively as possible.

I should say here that the process of reviewing your costs of living – along with the attendant requirement of living within your budget – requires some planning ability and good discipline. For some readers, the ability to budget and stick to that budget are second nature, often because they've learned to run a business. For others, it will be more challenging. And for those to whom this process is foreign, I recommend the services of a good local financial adviser. Usually a trusted tax accountant or attorney can suggest someone in your town for this purpose. Unless you have so much money that you don't have to think about budgeting (and sometimes even deca-millionnaires don't qualify for that kind of insouciance), making a personal or family budget and sticking to it are essential. If you need help to do so, get it.

Key Take-Away Points from Chapter 1:

- **Put the wonderful power of compounding to work for you as early in your life as possible. Begin a good investment program as soon as you can...don't put it off. The longer you can leave your money invested, the more your wealth will grow.**

- **The very first place you should put available investment dollars is to pay off any and all personal debts, with the possible exception of a thirty-year fixed rate mortgage on your primary and/or secondary residence (see Chapter 3). Not until all other debts are brought to zero and kept there should you invest in anything else.**

- **Be frugal: review your living costs and reduce them as much as possible. This will free up more of your income for investment on an on-going basis and will lead more quickly to your personal financial freedom.**

Chapter 2

Building an Investment Safety Net

Why Do You Need a Safety Net?

High wire acts normally use a "safety net" because, of course, they could fall and don't want to suffer the dire consequences of meeting the ground. Falling into the net during a performance might be a little embarrassing, but it beats falling to the floor with questionable odds of survival. Walking a high wire without a safety net may not mean the performer is clinically crazy, but it would definitely place him or her in the category of "extreme risk-taker".

In the same way, an investment safety net is absolutely mandatory for any investor who is not an extreme financial risk-taker.

Why? Let's consider two simple facts:

1. Of all the places where you could invest money (after paying off your debts), the two classes of investment that

can most powerfully grow your financial capital are (a) equities in (stocks of) good companies and (b) ownership of good real estate. I refer to them as the "Big Two," and they are the real engines of growth for personal wealth.

2. Unlike far less effective wealth growers (cash, CD's, T-bills, etc.), investments in the "Big Two" are, by their nature, volatile. Their prices vary…sometimes going way up and down. On top of volatility, with real estate you have investments that are usually not liquid (i.e., quickly convertible into cash.)

Therein lies the danger: volatility and illiquidity can lead to trouble if – and only if - you don't have an investment safety net. While we'll discuss better ways of building it, a safety net could be as simple as having enough money to live on for a few years tucked away in a money market account at a bank. If you have this, you can weather volatility and temporary illiquidity because the funds are there to support you if you need them - just like the safety net in the high wire act.

Let's look at what can happen if you do not have a safety net. Imagine that you had a good job in which you felt secure and you took every last cent you had and invested it in a portfolio (a group or "basket") of stocks. And let's give you credit for making smart choices, so this is a portfolio of good strong firms. Now let's assume that some unexpected shock hit the U.S. economic system and the value of your portfolio fell 50%. Maybe this doesn't happen in a day, but over a two- or three-year period, as it did in 2000-2002. To make matters worse, let's imagine that the malady precipitating the market downturn also puts enough financial pressure on your company that it has to cut back, and you lose your job. You may have good skills, but employers might not be hiring in the wake of this economic shock, and you need money to live on until the right job does become available. One place you can get it is to sell some – or maybe all - of your stocks. Perhaps that's the *only* place you can turn for the cash you need to cover your living expenses, since you have put everything you could into your purchase of these good companies. So you are forced to sell your stocks at a time when the price of your holdings has fallen 50%. You've gotten yourself into a real pickle:

1. You are selling your stocks at a low point...probably at prices considerably below their true fair value. Remember "Buy low, sell high"? You are being forced to do just the opposite, giving up what price appreciation you had gained previous to the 50% drop and having to realize, perhaps, some significant loss of your initial investment monies to boot. That's depressing enough, but...

2. When the market falls seriously, at some point it inevitably turns around and rises again. But before the turnaround, you were forced to *sell* your stocks at, possibly, the very best time to be *buying*.

   So you lose in two ways. Ugly. In a financial sense, you were walking a high wire, and are now meeting the ground.

Volatility

Isn't volatility awful? Isn't it shameful how stock prices can go up and down, sometimes radically and quickly? And if you think markets can be volatile, how about the prices of individual companies? They can gyrate wildly, sometimes not traceable to any specific economic event or change affecting the company or its on-going potential.

Isn't volatility awful? It may seem so on the surface, but no, it is most assuredly not. Be eternally grateful for volatility, because without it, you would never be able to buy the stock of good companies cheaply. "Buying low" is more than a cliché. It is the secret to maximizing your returns in equity ownership.

Let me give an example. A company I was following in 2002, called FactSet Research Systems (FDS), provides on-line integrated database services for financial companies. I believed the company's economics and management were superior and that it had a bright future for profit enhancement, so I bought it when I had a chance at $17.50 per share (split adjusted). Because of volatility, the market had offered what I considered to be an irresistible opportunity. I had calculated that shares were really worth something like $34 at that time. Imagine how excited you'd be to find a temporary half-price sale on a new car you wanted? Well, this kind of find is even better because it is, essentially, a half-price sale on an asset that actually *appreciates* in value. So, the volatility of the market created this wonderful opportunity. Since then FactSet's profits have grown nicely and its price is $62.85 as of March 31, 2007. That's 259% up in about 5 years. Volatility, my dear investor, should be your friend. It makes truly great returns and rapid wealth building possible.

Investing courses in most institutions of higher learning usually focus on a measure of investment risk called, simply, "Beta". Beta is the standard measure of volatility of a particular stock as it correlates to the volatility of the market as a whole. However, if you are a long-term investor, the big risk in investing is not volatility...whether it be market volatility or volatility in the price of an individual stock. If you are investing for a 5 to 10 year (or longer) period, you can wait out volatility (especially those nasty dips) easily. Rather, the risk you should care about is the possibility of permanent loss of capital in an investment. And one of the ways permanent loss of capital can occur is by being forced to sell holdings at a bad time, when prices are way down.

Given this truth, I believe that the preoccupation of American academia with volatility, and volatility's depiction as the definitive way to measure the "risk" of owning a particular stock, is a great disservice to impressionable young students. It is the wrong risk to focus on. Also, what do you think happens to the "Beta" of a company's stock when the price of that company falls from $50 to $25 in one day (maybe on some bad news and attendant fear)? Well, falling fast means it is more volatile, so its "Beta", of course, rises. And since "Beta" is a measure of risk, the academics would have you believe the stock is now riskier to buy. But, when the price of a stock gets cut in half, is it necessarily more risky to buy? To me, it is usually less risky to buy that company, all things being equal, than when it was much higher (100% higher) in price.

As long as you are a reasonably long-term investor, volatility is not an onerous risk. On the contrary, it is the key to investment opportunity. To get comfortable with volatility, you just have to make sure you can take advantage of it instead of it taking advantage of you. That's the difference, really, between the FactSet scenario, where I took advantage of volatility, and the example of the person forced to sell their stocks after a 50% drop in prices. You see, when they sold, someone was buying - someone was taking advantage of the volatility.

How do you make sure you are set up to take advantage of volatility? ***By having an adequate safety net.*** Clearly, if the unfortunate person who was temporarily out of work had some place to turn to cover their living expenses rather than selling their stocks, they could forgo the disastrous effects of a forced sale. For example, if they had annual living expenses of $100,000 and $300,000 in CD's tucked away, they could afford to hunt for a good job to replace the old one. And they would not be forced into selling any of their portfolio of strong companies. Now, you'll say, if it took three years to find a good job, then they will have depleted the safety net!

That's true. However, in the meantime, the value of their stocks has probably rebounded to yield considerably more than the original $300,000 in their safety net (depending on how quickly the market recovered and the size and quality of their investments.) Thus, they could sell some of their stock once the value had bounced back, and use the proceeds to replace their safety net, thus making them able to weather another possible storm in the future.

Now, how big your safety net should be is an important subject that we will cover later in this chapter, as well as other ways of creating a safety net besides using CD's.

I hope this example illustrates beyond a doubt the need for a safety net for all sane investors, but, as I speak with people these days, it's clear that some feel far too confident about their financial security. Since the 2001-2002 market downturn – serious by any realistic person's measure – things have been going very well in the markets. To review the facts, at the beginning of 2000 The Dow Jones Industrial Average hit about 12,000 and had fallen below 7300 in the later half of 2002. That's almost a 40% drop. Four years later it had climbed back to 12,000 again. That's a 64% gain - what it took just to return to "even" this time.

Now, you might think that most people would be traumatized enough by this deep and extended dip to make very sure a reasonable safety net was in place. But what I'm hearing among quite a few investors reflects complacency born of the fact that the pain of the steep drop was felt four years ago while the rosy feelings of a steady recovery have been with us, almost non-stop, ever since. It's kind of a comfortable naiveté, as I can almost hear some people thinking, "Well, yes, that happened back then, but everything's fine now…I talked with my broker the other day and I feel pretty optimistic."

Here's the grim reality: volatility is always with us and market corrections have happened with great regularity throughout the history of markets. So, if you're feeling sanguine, consider this: As of June 1, 2007, the financial press is trumpeting the fact that the Dow Jones Industrial Average is enjoying the second longest period in history without a "correction" (technically defined as a downturn of 10% or more in the index.) I figure that the longer we forgo a 10% correction, the higher the odds that the correction, when it inevitably comes, could be more than 10%.

Does this sound paranoid? Let's consider a few points. The housing industry, once fueled to frenzy by low interest rates and easily available loans, is being severely challenged and housing starts have fallen dramatically. The Fed has made 17 rate increases, yet the core inflation rate is near a 10-year high. Many say the federal budget deficit is out of control as we continue very expensive conflicts abroad, so we have rapidly growing domestic and foreign debt. Our trade deficit is huge. As baby boomers age, Social Security and Medicare liabilities loom. We have ample reason to believe that terrorists could be planning more attacks on U.S. soil. So, it's not all roses these days. To paraphrase one of Kissinger's great lines, just because you're paranoid doesn't mean you don't have enemies. When it comes to financial paranoia, not all the enemies are people.

Don't get me wrong. I invest without any particular fear of the things just enumerated. Plenty of good developments are underway that could continue the record number of market session days before a correction. But, unless we want to bury our collective heads in the sand, we need to admit that many factors which could possibly trigger a severe correction are in place. And the truth is, they always will be.

What you have to conclude from all this is that the only sensible way to invest is for the ***long-term,*** set up to be able to take advantage of tough times and not be a victim of them. You should be prepared to leave money in your investments for at least five years, preferably many more. Any time horizon of less than five years suggests you are gambling rather than investing.

Thus,

Smart Investing Step Three:

After your debts are paid off, the next place to invest your money is in the construction of a safety net that will insulate you from the negative effects of price volatility and allow you to become a long-term investor.

What Should Comprise Your Safety Net?

The concept of a safety net is not complex : it is simply having enough money set aside to tide you over during a financial "storm" A safety net must be:

1. Very liquid ***and***
2. Very safe

Exactly how much money you should dedicate to this safety net is covered in the next section. Here, I'll confine the discussion to the wisest construction of the net.

Safety nets necessarily have two components.

The first is a "cash pad" that is enough to take care of more immediate cash needs (based on your living expenses), including enough to handle unforeseen emergencies beyond normal living expenses (monies that you could call on if you suddenly and unexpectedly need to replace the roof on your house, for example.)

This "cash pad" is best kept in a totally liquid form, a combination of a checking account (hopefully one that will earn some interest) and a money market account. The money market rate will be higher than a checking account rate, so keep the bulk of your cash pad there. Also, you'll find it helpful to either have both of these accounts at the same bank, or to have the two accounts at different banks "linked," so that you can easily move money from one account to the other as needed.

The second component of the safety net: enough money to tide you over for a few years of living expenses (including an amount to handle unforeseen emergencies as you have in the immediate needs "cash pad".) Since inflation is also a reality of life, consider setting aside a bit more for each year as time goes on. Let's look at a simple situation.

If your living expenses are $100,000 for "year one" and you want to have a $10,000 in emergency slush fund available each year, you'll put aside $110,000 for year one, then, to allow for some inflation, $113,000 or a bit more for year two, $117,000 for year three, etc. It's the notion of having a certain amount earmarked for each year that gives us a "ladder" of sorts, with each year being a "rung" on the ladder. You might think of it as a "freedom ladder" because it gives you the freedom to invest in a long-term way – the only sensible way - without fear of dire consequences.

So, where do you invest the money to construct this ladder? You could just keep it in a money market account, but there are better places to put money - places that earn higher interest and are still quite safe. The most obvious of these is bonds. Bonds are simply promises, on behalf of a company, governmental agency or municipality, to pay back your principal upon a maturity date and, during the life of the bond, to pay interest.

Before describing which bonds are best-suited for a freedom ladder, let me say that we just came through a period where bond rates were so low that two things temporarily stopped me from buying bonds for my ladder:

1. The difference between the interest rates on high quality bonds (the only kind you should even consider) and money market rates was very small, and
2. The Fed was raising rates repeatedly to curb inflation, so it seemed likely that if I bought a bond, I would soon

be disappointed that I bought too early, as the rates on the new bonds available would be higher. If you buy a bond with a 4% yield (the interest rate paid) and a year from now similar bonds are offering a 5% yield, the resale value of that 4% bond will go down. That, in itself, didn't concern me, because I never plan to sell a bond. I'm only interested in seeing that my principal is returned when the bond matures. But I do mind forgoing the higher interest rates that will probably be available soon while we're in a definite interest-rate escalation.

So, in periods when the Fed is raising rates, you may want to hold off until rates seem to have stabilized, keeping your safety net funds in a money market account until that time.

Building a Freedom Bond Ladder Using Municipal Bonds

The type of bonds that are most well-suited for the bond ladder are high quality municipal bonds from your own home state. Why is that?

Municipal bonds are issued by state, county and city governments which use the money they borrow to build schools and bridges, hospitals and roads, or to improve infrastructure. The two big differences between municipal and corporate bonds:

1. The interest on municipal bonds is exempt from federal tax. Moreover, interest on municipal bonds issued *within your state* is exempt from state tax also. Some states don't even require that bonds you own be written in their state to be tax-exempt. If you are in the 28% federal tax bracket (the most common) and if you might pay another 5% (net) in state tax, that's a big advantage. However, in order to make

up for this advantage and attract capital, corporate bonds usually pay a higher rate. Typically, when you calculate the "post tax" rate, the differences between what you keep in interest income from high quality corporate bonds and high quality municipal bonds (issued at the same time and for comparable maturities) is small.

2. Corporate bonds are promises to pay interest, plus repay the amount of the bond when it matures and that's where I think municipal bonds have an edge over corporate bonds. What we are trying to build here, remember, is the big and important part of your safety net. And the most important thing about a safety net is that it be safe. The last thing you need is an economic downturn or shock to come along, precipitating your need to live off your safety net for a while, and the corporate bonds you used to build your bond ladder are virtually worthless because the company went bankrupt. Oh, you say, I'm being paranoid again... "Fortune 500" companies rarely go bankrupt. True, but, over the past few years, we've seen some very large companies leaving folks high and dry. So you may want to think twice before having the key part of your personal safety net in corporate bonds.

On the other hand, "revenue bonds" – one type of municipal bond - are backed by the underlying "business" (e.g., a toll road or city-owned utility company) to make good on the obligation. If you buy a high quality revenue bond, these bonds are generally very safe in my opinion. Even better are the "general obligation" bonds because they rely on the municipality's right to tax its citizens to cover interest and principal repayment. If a company gets overextended, it may declare bankruptcy. If a municipality gets overextended, it can just raise taxes. That's a comforting thought.

Not a Bond *Fund*

Please note that I am not talking about buying a bond ***fund or funds*** to build your ladder. There is a big difference between buying individual bonds – instruments which will mature on a given date and return your principal - and a bond fund.

Think of bond funds as mutual funds which own bonds. They buy and hold bonds of different types, but bond funds do not have a maturity date at which they promise to pay you back principal. It works very much like a stock mutual fund in that its value moves up and down over time, reflecting changes in the value of the underlying bonds as a result of changes in prevailing interest rates and demand for the bonds held by the fund. Perhaps you already glean the problem with them for our purposes of building the major component of a low-risk safety net.

Let's imagine a scenario when interest rates are on the rise. That would mean that the prices people will pay for previously issued bonds (issued during a time of lower interest rates) would go down. Why pay the same price for a 4% bond as is being asked for a 5% bond? You'd only consider buying it if it were cheaper in price, right? So as interest rates go up, buyers discount lower rate bonds - their prices go down.

So what if, just as the value of your bond fund is down, the day comes when you need to use the money in your safety net to live on for a while? If your bond ladder is not a bond ladder, but a laddered series of bond funds, you may be forced to sell some of the funds at a loss because their prices are down. That's just what you wanted to avoid in the first place: suffering the bad consequences of market volatility.

Under this same scenario, if instead of owning the bond funds, you own a ladder of good municipal bonds, interest rates can go up, and the price people are willing to pay for bonds can go down. Who cares? You are not going to sell the bonds. You are going to hold them through to maturity, at which point they will convert to cash at the full amount you were counting on.

So…

Don't use a bond fund or funds to construct any part of your safety net, and…

Don't sell bonds in your bond ladder; just let them mature.

Buying the Bond Ladder

How can you buy these bonds? It's pretty simple, as it turns out. Building on our previous example, you may want $110,000 to mature after one year, $113,000 to mature in two years, $117,000 in three years, etc. If you want to create a five-year bond ladder, for example, you buy enough bonds (enough in total "face value" as it is called…the amount paid at maturity) in each year so that they would fund your needs if you had to rely on your safety net to fund your living for some time. However, bonds are typically not available in "odd lots" (less than $10,000 increments). So if you want $113,000 you may have to put the last $3,000 in your money market account for safekeeping. Either way, you will have it available if and when you need it.

This "ladder" not only has the benefit of offering up what you need when you may need it, but it has two bonus features. First, if you get to the end of year one and the sky, financially speaking, has not fallen, then you just purchase a five-year bond with the proceeds of the year-one bond when it matures, thereby tacking one more "rung" onto the ladder, thus easily maintaining your five year safety net. Moreover, the interest the bonds have earned during the year will more than cover the increased cost of living you would normally add into the new "year five rung" calculation, without having to add more cash. It's wonderfully self-perpetuating.

Second, because you are making these purchases of additional "rungs" at yearly intervals (presuming you do not need the money when the bond matures) if interest rates ***do*** rise, you will be buying higher yield bonds as you tack on "rungs" from one year to the next. If rates fall, your ladder strategy will help because longer-term bonds in the portfolio will continue to pay the higher rate of interest.

When it comes to actually purchasing these bonds, you can either do it yourself or have someone do it for you. Since you are a busy person, you presumably won't want to deal with this, so let's discuss what it takes to have someone capable do it for you.

If you have a financial adviser or money manager who you trust, that's wonderful. If not, your accountant can probably refer you to someone who could handle this for you. It is neither difficult nor time-consuming to oversee the construction and maintenance of the ladder. However, you want to make sure it is done correctly, following four simple guidelines in buying the bonds for your ladder.

1. There are states in which some of the bonds are shaky (and, therefore, low-rated), but if you can get high-rated bonds in your state, it is usually best to do so in order to avoid paying state tax on the interest income[1].

2. Bonds rated below these "Investment Grade" levels are speculative in nature and do not belong anywhere near your safety net. Standard and Poor's rate "Investment Grade" bonds using this scale:

AAA	Highest Quality
AA	High Quality
A	Tier 1 – Medium
BBB	Tier 2 – Medium

[1] It should be noted that residents of some states, such as Indiana, are allowed state tax deductibility on municipal bonds issued by other states.

Moody's, the other prominent bond rating agency, uses slightly different codifications, but the risk ratings are essentially the same:

Aaa	Highest Quality
Aa	High Quality
A-1, A	Tier 1 – Medium
Baa-1, Baa	Tier 2 – Medium

My advice: ***buy only AA or Aa and AAA or Aaa bonds.*** One other thing: bond ratings can change. Something that's "AA" today may be downgraded if the rating agency considers the municipality's ability to repay has weakened due to it getting overextended issuing bond debt. The safest route is to buy bonds which are insured (that is, if the municipality is unable to pay up when the bond matures, the insurer steps in and pays you.) It doesn't get much safer than that.

3. Avoid hospital bonds. Revenue bonds that are issued to build hospitals have one problem. Hospitals are essentially single-purpose facilities. If the hospital doesn't make it financially, the building normally can't be used for anything else, and bond holders could be left holding the bag!

4. Pay attention to if and when the bonds are "callable" (when they can be paid off prior to maturity by the municipality.) If, in your ladder, you are counting on a bond to mature in a certain year, you don't want to be surprised by having it called early. A callable bond is likely to be called early if interest rates go down after the municipality issues the bond. In essence, they will want to refinance with cheaper debt, just as you might refinance your home to take advantage of lower interest rates. What is the harm if this happens (e.g., the bond is called two years before

you expected it to mature)? Well, nothing awful…it's just inconvenient to have to fill in the missing part of the bond value for the year in which you were expecting it to mature. And the interest rate at which you can do so will almost always be lower than the one you had.

So, when would a money manager not be "willing and able" to follow these guidelines? If what they normally do in buying bonds is something quite different. So, as you talk with a few money managers, ask them how they normally build bond ladders – what guidelines they use - and see if their thinking is in line with the above parameters. Some reasons why a particular money manager might not be right for this job:

- They buy both high- and lower-rated (below AA) bonds
- They like to "trade" bonds, to buy and sell them, trying to anticipate which way interest rates are headed
- They might favor selling some of your bonds before they fully mature if their value has gone up

If, in talking with people whom you are vetting as potential bond managers, you hear these kinds of things, I suggest you move on to someone else. It is important to get this right.

Once you find someone with whom you feel comfortable, tell them the general purpose of the ladder and lay out – in writing, preferably – the amount you would like to come due in each year (rung) of the ladder. By the way, maybe you would prefer to have each year's rung come due on, let's say, September first of each year, but good bonds maturing in the year you're trying to "fill" may not mature on September 1, so you should be prepared to be somewhat flexible about this.

Next, give the manager the instructions; specifically: (1) purchase only "AA"/"Aa" or "AAA"/"Aaa" rated bonds, ***preferably***

insured, (2) purchase bonds issued by municipalities within your state if possible, (3) avoid hospital bonds, and (4) avoid bonds that are callable "early." Make it clear that you will never sell your bonds, but will just let them go to maturity. And, as long as you find it unnecessary to tap the bond ladder for living expenses, you want the manager to add a "rung" to the end of the ladder each year as a year's worth of bonds mature and their proceeds become available.

If they understand these specifications, all should be well. What, in dollar terms, will it cost to have this done? It depends on the amount of money you need in your bond ladder, and the rate the manager wants to charge. These days it could be as low as about 1/4 of one percent or "25 basis points" per year (100 "basis points" equals one full percent) for a large bond ladder. And for a small ladder, the annual cost could be as high as one percent (100 basis points.)

As an example, if your adviser constructed a bond ladder totaling $2 million and charged 25 basis points annually, this task would cost $5,000 per year.

Prefer to do it yourself and save the money? If you have the time (and it doesn't require much), use a discount brokerage firm to help you buy and keep custody of your bond portfolio. Specialists at their "bond desk" can help you through all the particulars if you tell them what you're trying to do. But be sure to take enough time to clearly convey that you want to do a bond ladder, how much you want to mature in each year, how many years long you want it, and the specific bond guidelines discussed above.

In some cases, they may need to explain a "pre-refunded" bond or the difference between current yield and the yield to maturity, and other minutiae, but most bond desks – as long as they understand what you are trying to do – are very helpful. They will bring various bonds to your attention, describing their ratings, what type of bond they are (a school bond, a bond to build a new toll bridge, etc.), what their call provisions are, what their price and effective yield is, the amount of the bonds available to be purchased, etc. Then you make decisions filling in your ladder by keeping track of the totals you need each year until each is "filled".

How Big Should Your Safety Net Be?

This is an important question, and an area where I see some otherwise intelligent people behaving, shall we say, inadvisably. Make sure you get it right. The first part of the safety net is pretty straightforward; it's the second part where people make costly – sometimes very costly - mistakes.

The "Cash Pad"

Let's start by considering the first component of the safety net: the "cash pad". What you want in cash or cash equivalents (checking account, savings account, or money market) is enough to pay (1) your living expenses for the immediate future, and (2) unexpected expenses that may come up (a repair bill you weren't expecting, your share of the costs of an unexpected wedding, etc.)

Set aside, in readily available cash, whatever makes you totally comfortable. I put a full year's cash needs for living in the cash pad at the beginning of every year so I won't have to spend any time mid-year pulling money from my investments.

Be sure you anticipate ***all*** of your living expenses - not only mortgage or rent payments, utilities, and clothing purchase needs for you and your family, but all the other things you will need, including, but not limited to, money you will spend on:

- Vacation travel/ trips to visit children or have them visit you
- Grocery/drugstore purchases
- Dining out
- Spousal and/or child support payments
- Entertainment (going to a movie, a sports event, buying books and music, etc.)
- Gasoline/oil changes/servicing and maintenance/car washes/ registration expense
- Insurance - health, cars, home, liability umbrella, long-term care, jewelry and art riders, workman's compensation (if you employ household help or a gardener, for example) etc.
- Charity gifts /gifts for holidays and birthdays/anniversaries for family/friends
- Medical expenses and the costs of medicine (both over the counter and prescriptions) not covered by your health insurance, including dental, orthodontic, eye doctor, etc.
- Cleaning – house, dry-cleaning and laundry
- Dues to a homeowners association, clubs, etc.
- Subscriptions
- Memberships (golf club, gym, etc.)
- Personal grooming (barber, hairdresser, etc.)
- TV cable/Internet/phone
- Home related items: garden supplies and plant materials/ heating/air conditioning service/ security system monitoring/ miscellaneous repairs and maintenance/pest control/trash removal/window cleaning/pool or pond maintenance/snow removal and lawn and tree maintenance
- Education-related expenses
- Allowances to your children
- Major gifts to your children (like annual allowable amounts to trust funds)
- Money you pay your children for work they do (some or all of which they could invest in their Roth IRA,)

- Expenses associated with ownership of things, like a boat or RV
- Costs of your children's sporting activities
- Pet food, vet, grooming, and pet-sitting

Also, take into account expenses that come up somewhat predictably, but not yearly. For example, you may have to paint your house about every five years. It's prudent to accrue one-fifth of the cost of the paint job each year tucking it away so that you can access the funds when it's time.

The cash pad should also, as we have said, include an amount to handle expenses you cannot anticipate, because emergencies do happen. How much should you include for contingencies? Again, it's whatever makes you comfortable. And the costs of emergencies that can occur differ depending upon your life. For example, the cost of replacing a roof on a $3,000,000 home is a lot different than it is on a small home. Just include an amount that you feel is ample.

The Bond Ladder

Now you have the cash you need for a year of living, plus emergencies, at hand. You are ready to go to the second component of the safety net: the "Freedom Bond Ladder." Here again, you want to have enough money maturing in each year to make you comfortable that you'd be fine if you needed to live off of the proceeds of that ladder for a while (i.e., the bond principal that matures each year; ***not*** the interest.) So you want to anticipate your living expenses going forward as best you can, and do it conservatively. It's better to err to the high side.

First, look at the total living expenses you have now. You can get a pretty good idea of these by looking at what you actually spent over the last 12 months. If you spend everything out of your checkbook, including paying your credit card bills and generating checks for cash you need, a careful review of the amounts you wrote during the past twelve months will give you a good idea of the cash outflow. You may also have some cash *inflow* that you need to subtract from your estimate. If you pay for company travel on your personal credit card and then get reimbursed by your company for that travel, for example, you need to add back the total of those re-imbursements when calculating your net cash outflow for your *personal* living expenses. Make sense?

Once you've estimated your total personal living expenses, it's advisable to project future years' needs with two things in mind:

1. The year-to-year increase in the cost of living, and
2. Changes in your life that will trigger changes in what it costs you to live.

The cost of living, as reflected in the Consumer Price Index, has increased about 3% per year on average over the past 100 years, so you may want to take your base figure of living needs up each year by 3%. After you buy your initial bond ladder, however, the expense associated with the rising cost of living can be taken care of by the interest your bonds generate. As you roll forward from year to year, adding an additional year to your ladder (in order to keep the length of the ladder constant), you can just use the interest earnings to add some to the principal each year.

Anticipated changes in your life could mean you'll need more money in certain years, and perhaps less in others. A couple of examples: if you have a son or daughter graduating from high school who is headed to college, you'll need to add an amount you feel is safe to cover tuition, books, room, board and allowance. If, on the other hand, the kids are successfully out on their own now and you and your wife plan to sell your palatial estate and move into a cozy little bungalow that costs considerably less to maintain, you may be scaling back your living costs in a number of areas. That could make a sizable difference in what you'll need after the move is made.

Only you can look into your future to be able to project changes in living needs and only you can say when you are comfortable with the amounts you are going to set aside in the bond ladder to hold you over if and when things get bad for a while.

By now you should have a clear idea of what you need in future years and you've been conservative in estimating those needs, knowing it's hard to get in trouble having a bit too much money maturing each year. The question is, how many years of the ladder should you buy?

That all depends on your life situation and, generally speaking, there are two "camps" in which you might find yourself at this moment: "Camp 1" or Camp 2". If you are like most folks, you will move from "Camp 1" to "Camp 2" at some point in your life, so even if you are in "Camp 1" now, take a moment to read about "Camp 2" so you understand the difference and its implications.

Camp 1

Camp 1 is comprised of people who would have relatively little trouble covering their living expenses if bad times hit. Who are these people?

First there are the young mobile professionals who have skills that are in high demand. Even when these people lose their jobs because of the failure of a start-up company or lay-off, they will most likely get another good job soon. I have nephews and nieces in Camp 1 and I am constantly amazed at the nonchalance they display when talking about the possibility that a job might end. It's just a fact of life for them and, while inconvenient, not terribly threatening. A new good job will not take a long time for them to find.

Another group is people for whom the threat of losing a job is remote. These are people who own their own businesses or are partners in good businesses. If the market and their holdings dropped 30% in a year, they wouldn't like it, and in a bad business environment their "owner's earnings" (the actual cash earnings they could expect to take home) might be reduced. But they wouldn't miss a beat covering their living costs, which could still be easily covered by their business proceeds. They may have to cut back on the number of vacations to Europe or the like, but they are not going to starve.

There are other people who are, at least temporarily, in Camp 1. Camp 1 is really defined by the fact that you don't need a big, long bond ladder because you are not likely to have a long interruption in your normal earned income stream. Some Camp 1 campers might feel comfortable having just a year or two in their "Freedom Bond Ladder." Some might feel comfortable having a little more, but a 6 to 10 year ladder would clearly be overkill.

I've been an entrepreneur for a long time, but I still like having a big safety net with a long bond ladder. I am clearly a risk-averse personality when it comes to things that could threaten my - and my family's - livelihood.

I know one person who probably doesn't need any bond ladder at all. His business is so profitable and so well defended against competition (by strong barriers to entry), and he has such total control of staying "employed", that the right ladder length for him would probably be zero years. Such people are rare. And happy.

Camp 2

A camper here would have considerably more trouble covering his or her living expenses if bad times hit. Who are they? Quite a few different types reside in this camp:

- People whose skills are not so superb, rare, or in demand that, if they lost their jobs, they'd be working again in no time. It will take a while for them to find a great job.

- People who may be in top-level management of businesses, but don't own so much of the companies for which they work that they couldn't be laid off or fired.

- People who do own enough of a business that they couldn't be fired, but that business is not so vastly profitable, or so well competitively-defended, that they can be assured an income stream that will easily cover their living costs if tough times occur. This is especially true if they live expensively.

- People who have little or no yearly income from a job (relative to their living costs) because they are:

    - Retired, living principally off their investments and the "passive" income these produce.

    - Working in a job they love that doesn't cover all their living expenses (and they are, therefore, partially dependant on their investments to live.)

    - Working in a non-paying job—perhaps volunteering for a non-profit or caring for their families full-time. If they are single parents, they may be receiving child and spousal support, but when times are tough, that income stream could be threatened.

How *Long* a Ladder?

Obviously, folks in Camp 1 need, in most cases, a shorter ladder than those in Camp 2. What ladder is long enough for you? It has to be one you are comfortable with, based on your situation and your personal feelings of risk aversion.

In a broad sense, the prudent range for Camp 1 residents – as long as they stay in Camp 1 - is from two to five years at most. If you feel more than five years is necessary for some reason, you may really be a Camp 2 camper.

Camp 2 residents should probably be in the five- to ten-year range. More than ten years, in most cases, would be overkill. Even if you derive all the money you need for living expenses from investments (i.e., you have no income that is "earned" through a job), ten years gives the markets a very long time to come back. And, if you purchase your assets using the principles of investing in this book, your portfolio is likely to perform better than most even when the market is declining.

But the decision has to be yours. If you won't sleep well at night unless you have a twelve-year ladder, then that is what is right for you. Reading the next section will make you keenly aware of the downside of such a long ladder, but you have to do what makes you comfortable. If you're not comfortable, you will never be able to have the right attitude about investing in the "Big Two" wealth-building engines - the long-term perspective and emotionally-detached attitude of smart investors. And if you don't have the right attitude but you do it anyway, you may make costly mistakes, as many do.

Avoid Putting More Than You Need Into the Bond Ladder

Bonds are great for building a good safety net, as we've discussed, but there is something you should know about bonds:

if you are interested in investments that will make your wealth grow nicely, bonds are not that. They are a good alternative for most people to cash or cash equivalents for the safely net, but that's all they are good for. As wealth-growing investments, they are not good at all. Let's examine the grounds for that opinion.

Imagine you bought a 10-year bond that yielded 4.5% annually and you paid $1,000 for it, which was the face amount of the bond (i.e. the amount the bond issuer agrees to pay at the end of ten years). That bond would pay $45 each year and then, at maturity, the entity that issued the bond would repay you the $1,000 face amount.

Assuming the inflation rate is running at its historical average of roughly 3%, you have a little problem. That $1,000 returned to you at the end of year ten, when discounted at 3% for ten years, is the equivalent of only $737 in today's money! That is, it will only buy you about 74% of what it would buy when you bought the note. What kind of wealth growth is that? This investment has dropped in value over 26% in ten years!

Roger Ibbotson's data shows how bad bonds are as investments. Looking at seventy-five years of Ibbotson's data, if you put $1,000 into Treasury Bills at the end of 1925, by the year 2000 you would have ended up with **seventeen** times your money. Now, if you bought longer-term bonds instead (meaning you would have assumed a bit more risk), you would have wound up with **forty-nine** times your money. The *inflation-adjusted* return, as we know, would have been a whole lot less, but let's continue comparing apples and apples.

U.S. stocks (just the general market, never mind particularly intelligent investment strategies) returned **2,600** times your money over that same period.

There is just no comparison.

As Gary Belsky and Thomas Gilovich said in their informative book, *Why Smart People Make Big Money Mistakes*, "That's the irony of the so called conservative investment strategy: it is arguably more risky (and reckless) to leave yourself vulnerable to the ravages of inflation than it is to subject yourself to the hills and valleys of the stock market."

"Vulnerable to the ravages?," you ask, "What's so ravaging about 3% inflation?" Well, you've seen that even 3% inflation can make bond investments pretty marginal as wealth growers. But what would have happened to the value of your bonds if we returned to a period like the 1970s? Look at the rates of inflation for the ten years from 1972 to 1981:

1972	3.41%
1973	8.80%
1974	12.20%
1975	7.01%
1976	4.81%
1977	6.77%
1978	9.03%
1979	13.31%
1980	12.40%
1981	8.94%

Ah, the good old days! In this scary scenario, your safety net bond ladder would be fine for two reasons.

- First, you would never sell your bonds on the open market; you would wait for them to mature, receiving the full face amount each year that you'd planned for, so the falling market would not affect what you realized out of the bonds.

- Second, as years went by and you rolled over proceeds from one year's maturing bonds to add a year to the ladder, you would average up to the higher-than-historical rates and that would give you considerably better yield. But if you owned a lot of bonds as ***investments***, hoping to profit from the rise in their prices, you would have been crushed (as interest rates rise, the price of bonds falls.) And what if you were in retirement with a big investment in "safe" bonds?

A Drawback of the "Asset Allocation" Approach: Over-Investing in Bonds

Most investment advisers use some sort of asset allocation model which, taking into account your age and life situation, seeks to put a certain percent of your money in nice safe income-producing securities like bonds, and a certain percent in what they consider the "riskier" (read: "more volatile") investments, such as stocks. Advisers usually have their own preferred models; these models may also take factors into account such as your risk tolerance, how expensively you live, etc. A model might suggest, for example, that the percent asset allocation for a certain retired individual, given the person's lifestyle, age, and risk tolerance, is 40% bonds / 60% stocks and real estate investments. Nice and safe, right? But what if that individual was quite wealthy and had, say, $12 million in net worth, of which $10 million represented assets that could be invested. The asset allocation suggests this investor should invest $4 million in bonds.

To keep the example simple, let's assume that this investor has a cost of living of $200,000 per year and $200,000 is exactly the amount he or she wants to mature each year in his or her safety net bond ladder. Let's further assume that the investor feels totally comfortable with a seven-year bond ladder. Well, then, the size of the bond ladder would be seven years times $200,000, or $1.4 million dollars.

Clearly the "percent of assets" allocation approach will cause this investor to invest $2.6 million ***more*** in bonds than really necessary. This $2.6 million is needlessly growing as slowly as cold molasses running uphill while being exposed to the ravages of inflation that could sink its investment value all the while. The investor could have put this $2.6 million to work owning shares of some of the best businesses in the world - businesses that could raise prices to counter the effects of inflation. Or the $2.6 million could be invested in great real estate. If you are a wealthy person, in other words, the "assets allocation model", applied blindly, may lead you to invest far more in bonds than is smart.

Here's what does seem smart to me:

Invest in bonds only to the extent that you need them to build the bond ladder of your safety net...and then <u>not a penny more.</u> If this amounts to 50% of your investable assets or 5%, it does not matter. Calculate specifically what you need and buy a bond portfolio to match.

In the most poignant example I've read of how detrimental over-investing in bonds can be, Christopher Browne in his excellent *Little Book of Value Investing* tells the story of a widow whose husband died prematurely in 1947, leaving her $1,000,000:

> *To ensure a steady income for (her), the bank invested the estate in tax-exempt municipal bonds yielding 4 percent. An annual income of $40,000 per year in 1947 left her on easy street. However, no one thought she would live for another 55 years, which she did. When she died in 2002, she still had $40,000 per year income, but it was worth a lot less than it had been in 1947. I calculated that if her original $1 million had been invested in the S&P 500 stock index, and that if she had been allowed to spend 4% of the assets every year, by 1998 (the year that I did this little exercise), she would have had $44 million and an annual income of $1,760,000.*

Camp 2 Revisited

Retirees in Camp 2 need to think about that little story. If I were retired and had zero income apart from income from my investments, I certainly would not want to squander my investable assets this way, would you? Let's look for a moment at the case of another well-to-do retired couple who have living expenses of $300,000 per year, having no earned income, and having investable assets of $10 million. They could handle their investment approach in one of two ways:

1. They could put enough money into "safe" bonds to yield the after-tax equivalent of their living expenses each year, as we posited in a similar example in Chapter Two. To yield $300,000, they would need about $9.3 million in bonds (assuming they bought 4.5% yield Treasury notes, as we did in that example.) That leaves them just $700,000 to put into the great wealth growth engines of stocks and real estate. Or...

2. They could buy $300,000 in bonds each year of a ten-year bond ladder, dedicating $3,000,000 of their investable assets to that purpose. This would leave them $7 million to put into stocks and real estate to build their wealth powerfully and counter the effects of inflation...***ten times*** the amount they would put to work in the first case!

   If tough times come along in the market and they can't take $300,000 out of their investments in some years, that's OK. Their safety net will take care of them. Then, when the market improves, they can replenish missing rungs of the ladder.

So…

Smart Investing Step Four:

If you find yourself owning bonds above and beyond what you need for a safety net that makes you comfortable, liquidate them.

Before we go on, let's see where you are. Let's say you have calculated what you need in your safety net and that's all the money you have. You have no more money to put into equities and real estate. That's fine; you should put the safety net in place (or all of it that you can) and stop right there. If you want to invest in a way that sets you up to escape dire consequences in a severe market downturn (and I sincerely hope you do), you should not be investing in stocks and real estate (for investment purposes) yet. As you get additional money to invest, you can put that money toward these growth engines. Once the safety net is fully in place, you have prepared yourself to invest intelligently as a long-term investor who is able to withstand market volatility.

If you are in this situation, take heart! The next chapter may give you an additional source of investable assets that makes sense. If it does not, I would suggest you make a plan to put aside some of your earnings each month or each quarter and slowly get into "Step Five" with those savings. You may also have a windfall in the future through inheritance or other means which allows you to take advantage of your prepared situation and start acquiring the "Big Two" asset classes.

Who Might Not Need a Fully Funded Bond Ladder?

Is there anyone who does not need a safety net in place before moving on to "Step Five"? I think only two types of people can afford to be without a safety net entirely and then only for as long as they are in this enviable position:

1. A student who receives virtually all of his or her support from parents.

2. The lucky person who owns a firm that throws off owner's earnings that cover, perhaps many times over, his or her cost of living. Let me specify that this needs to be a firm that has excellent competitive advantages and that those advantages need to be sustainable (i.e., they won't dissipate when a better mousetrap comes along.)

Now, a more interesting question: Are there people who don't need fully-funded rungs in their bond ladder to be safe? If your living expenses totaled $100,000, for example, is there a situation in which you might feel comfortable having the bond ladder rungs only being $75,000 or $50,000? There are people like this who can afford to put more into stocks and real estate because the total required in the bond ladder is smaller.

One such person would be someone who owns a business that throws off owner's earnings that more than covers his or her living costs at the present time. The business is strong enough that if hard times came he or she would be hurt, but, at the very worst, take-home cash would be reduced to, say, $60,000. This person is not totally immune to an economic downdraft, but is partially immune to it. If this investor wanted, say, six years of protection in a Freedom Bond Ladder, he or she might be able to get away with dedicating $360,000 to that (six times $60,000), rather than $600,000.

Another person who might not need a fully-funded bond ladder is someone who has two income sources: one from work and one from an annuity, a trust, or spousal support (from an "ex" who is financially and morally solid). Even if this person lost his or her job, he or she might feel very confident about being able to cover living expenses. The same could be said of a spouse in a household where both adults are working. In these cases, the bond ladder might be able to be scaled back some, freeing more funds to go to the investment engines.

The safety net has to be what makes you feel comfortable. My advice: Search your heart, invest what you have to in the bond ladder to be totally secure, and no more. And remember, although you probably would have to change things rarely if at all, the bond ladder *can* be changed. If at some point in the future, you want to add to or subtract from a year's bond total because you learn that your needs are going to change, you are free to buy more bonds whenever you like, or sell some when there is a favorable climate.

Credit Where Credit Is Due

It's been said that there are no new ideas in life; only a new arrangement or new adaptation of old ones. All the ideas in this book probably had their roots somewhere and in many cases I couldn't tell you where. Some of the more important thoughts about investing can be attributed originally to someone and, when it can, I like to give credit where it is due. We owe innovative investors a lot for their legacy of intelligent thinking about investment because we can all benefit from it. I felt so strongly appreciative in the case of Warren Buffett that I wrote him a thank you letter back in 2001, to which he was kind enough to respond graciously.

For many of the guiding and powerful principles about equity investing, the names associated with the ideas are legend (at least, in investment circles), but I first started to grasp the need for a safety net in a discussion with a fellow you probably have not heard of. His name is Michael Stolper and he is a financial adviser and money manager in San Diego, CA. We met in the mid-90s and he talked about setting aside money in very safe instruments so that you could weather the market in bad times. This was the very worst time I could have received that advice, because it meant that I was going to have to forgo putting a sizable portion of my available assets into the market in what turned out to be one of the greatest bull runs in history. The Dow Jones average in 1994 was just under 4,000 (hard to believe!) and by the year 2000 it had run up to nearly 12,000, as we've discussed. Smart people and idiots alike made vast amounts of money in the later part of the 90's. Note: Never be impressed by somebody's track record if the period he or she is citing includes the late 90s!

There were, certainly, days in late 1999 that I wished I'd never met Michael and heard his advice, but it just made good sense so I stuck with it. Then came the days in 2000 through 2002 when I was so grateful that I'd followed his counsel! The market tanked (down about 40% in all over the three years) and my safety net was there to protect me. In the long run, the veracity – and the sagacity – of Michael's recommendation were clearly confirmed.

Even better, from 2000 to 2002, when most other people were seeing significant portions of their equity investment portfolios evaporate, the investments that I had made, following the principles you'll read about in the ensuing chapters of this book, went ***up***, not down.

Key Take-Away Points from Chapter 2:

- **To be prepared properly to invest in the "Big Two" wealth-growing engines of equities and real estate, you must** have an adequate safety net. If you do not, the volatility in prices that is the nature of these assets could cause you great financial harm.

- With the correct safety net in place you can become a long-term investor, able to take wise advantage of price volatility instead of being harmed by it.

- The safety net has two components: the "cash pad" for your short-term needs (over the next year, for example) and the "Freedom Ladder" to hold you over for as long as you judge adequate.

- Consider using municipal bonds (but not municipal bond *funds)* to construct your ladder. Generally, you want to purchase bonds:

    - From your own state
    - Rated AAA or AA, preferably insured
    - That are not hospital bonds, and
    - That are not callable early

- The design of the bond ladder – both the amount of bonds purchased in each year and the number of years in the ladder – is whatever makes you comfortable for your personal situation.

- Invest in bonds only to the extent that you need them to build your bond ladder. Don't put a penny more into bonds.

- If you find yourself with ownership of bonds above and beyond what you need for a safety net that makes you comfortable, liquidate them and use them to invest in the "Big Two"—equity and real estate.

Chapter 3

The Mortgage Question

When a Mortgage (or Two) Makes Sense

Chapter 2 outlined why most debt is bad for your financial health and should be paid off...not just the sky-high interest rates associated with credit card debt and cash loans against a credit card, but even car loans and other types of personal debt. The reasons to forgo car loan debt were:

1. The interest rate, while nowhere near a credit card's, is still high enough to give one pause because it is impossible to be sure you can do better than the interest rate of a car loan (about 7%) with your investments in the short run (say a four- or five-year time frame), and car loans are normally made for a short run time frame.

2. The government does not help you with your interest payments on car loans; the interest on such loans is not tax-deductible.

What about a mortgage on your primary residence and or a second home? This type of debt is a different story. The government allows you to deduct the annual interest on up to $1 million of aggregate loans—on either your primary or secondary residence, or on both together - if the mortgages were originally taken on as debt used to acquire the home or homes. You can also deduct the interest on up to $100,000 on a home equity line of credit.

This means you could potentially borrow, or have borrowed, up to $1.1 million for either your home or a combination of your homes. The government will pay a big chunk of the interest on those loans for you – an amount equal to your marginal federal plus state tax rate – as long as the mortgage is taken as original acquisition debt (not something you did after buying the house.) So this starts to be an interesting possibility.

It gets a whole lot more interesting when interest rates charged for mortgages are low, as they have been recently. Home mortgages are generally costing between 5.9 and 6.4% APR (Annual Percentage Rate.) The APR is a figure that expresses the total finance charge on a loan over its entire term. It includes the interest rate, fees, points, and mortgage insurance, and is therefore a more complete measure of a loan's cost than the just interest rate. If the APR is 6.3%, let's say, the actual interest rate (excluding the amortized amount for fees, points and mortgage insurance) would be about 6.1% on a 30-year fixed rate mortgage. That 6.1% represents what the government is going to allow you to deduct.

What is the ***after tax equivalent*** of a 6.1% interest rate if your combined federal and state tax is, let's say, 33%? It would be 6.1 times .67 (1.00 less .33), or 4.09%. On top of that, if you want to figure the hurdle rate you have to beat with your investments to justify holding the mortgage and using the proceeds to invest, you have to add back the 0.2%, roughly, associated with fees, points, and mortgage insurance over the life of the loan. The key question is: Is it reasonable to assume that you can achieve, over the life of the loan, better than a 4.3% return on your investments?

The big bugaboo that was present with car loans – their short term nature – and the attendant inability to be sure of beating the cost of the car loan in the short term with investment results, goes away as long as you get the right type of home loan. If you get 30-year fixed mortgages with no balloon payments due in the future, and you are prepared and happy to keep that mortgage in place over the long term, then your question becomes:

Can I do better than a 4.3% return with my investments over a long period?

Are you shouting "Yes!"? Well, maybe.

If you are ***prepared*** to invest all of the money from the loan in equities and real estate, then I'd say you have the right answer. Even if you did not use the advice in this book to produce superior results – even if you just threw the money into a stock index fund – you might reasonably expect, based on the long-term historical returns on stocks, to handily beat that 4.3% hurdle after taxes on your gains and dividends. And if you read the rest of this book and by putting its principles to work are fortunate enough to average 15% per year on your investments over the period, you would achieve an after-tax rate of return over the long haul far greater than 4.3%. (As long as you avoid a lot of turnover in your account and the resulting capital gains taxes.)

When Carrying a Mortgage May Not Make Sense

Notice I started that last paragraph "If you are ***prepared*** to invest…" What if you had enough money to pay off all of your credit card and other types of debt, but did ***not*** have enough to build the safety net that's right for you without using proceeds from this mortgage debt? Without a safety net, as you know, you should not be in stocks or real estate at all (yet). Using the proceeds of your mortgage to invest in stocks or real estate—and skipping construction of your safety net—would be high-risk behavior indeed.

O.K., you say, I'll use the proceeds to fund my safety net, and then put any remaining money into stocks and real estate. Let's think about that.

To make the math easy, let's say your total mortgage proceeds are $1 million. Let's also say that you have done it all right: 30-year fixed-rate mortgage(s), good low interest rate, no balloons, only on your primary and/or secondary residences, all debt being taken on as original acquisition debt when you bought the home or homes. Let's further posit that you will need to put $500,000 into your safety net (the cash pad plus the bond ladder). Depending how much of the safety net is in the cash pad (which pays little after-tax interest) and how much is in bonds (which pays somewhat better after-tax interest) you might be earning an after-tax income from interest on those assets of 3.5 to 4.0%.

Let's stop right here to make a point. If your safety net is going to require *all* the proceeds from your mortgage to complete it, either because the safety net needs are big (like $1 million) *<u>or</u>* the amount you can reasonably borrow in a 30-year fixed-rate mortgage on your home is not greater than what you need for the safety net (like $500,000), then this is a lousy bet, isn't it? You'll be paying about 4.3% with all costs of the mortgage considered, but you'll only be making 3.5%. That's a money-loser; not a wealth-builder.

OK, back to the scenario where you get $1 million in mortgage proceeds on your home, paying a total of 4.3% to do so. You invest half into your safety net, where you expect to make an after-tax return of 3.5 to 4.0%. You are going to put the rest into stocks of good companies.

Over a long period, what could you reasonably expect to make on the equity investments ***after taxes***? A conservative estimate might be at least 6%. So now you have half of the proceeds from the mortgage making 6% and half the proceeds making 3.5%. That 3.5% is a guess, too, because interest rates could sink back down again, or rise over the long haul. But if you have half in each side of the investment picture, you might expect to average something in the neighborhood of 4.7%; a very "iffy" 4.7%.

I don't think I'd take that bet - given this scenario I'm not confident that I could beat the 4.3% hurdle rate that the mortgage is going to cost. And during the years when my returns on investments are not so good, making the mortgage payments could be challenging.

Bottom Line

Taking on a mortgage when you purchase a home makes sense for two types of people:

1. People who, without a mortgage, could not afford to buy a home. Homes are good investments in many ways, and mortgages make homeownership possible for the majority of Americans who couldn't otherwise be homeowners.

2. People who don't need a mortgage, have plenty of money to fund an adequate safety net, and have additional funds to invest in stocks and real estate (without ***having*** to use mortgage proceeds). This scenario is not "iffy"; it would be prudent to take the mortgage (or not pay off the one(s) you already have.) Presuming you can get a low-cost 30-year fixed mortgage when you originally buy your home or

homes, the cost of the mortgage will be pretty easy to beat with equity investments over the long term. The mortgage proceeds, for these people, just add fuel to the fire of their wealth building, particularly if they have the financial capacity to carry the mortgage during an extended rough period. If, without the mortgage proceeds, they have, say, $2 million in equity and real estate assets, a $1.1 million dollar infusion from a mortgage now puts a full 55% more to work for them in the "Big Two" growth engines.

Now that you understand the need for a safety net, you can see that although carrying a mortgage or mortgages is great in some situations, it is not right for everyone.

Key Take-Away Point from Chapter 3:

- **If you can fund your safety net fully with monies other than mortgage proceeds, then it is prudent to *keep* a mortgage (or mortgages) – or *take* an original acquisition mortgage—up to $1 million on your primary and secondary residences (combined) and up to $100,000 in a home equity line of credit. This is only true if you are going to use that money to increase what you will invest in the "Big Two" wealth-building engines of equities and real estate. Otherwise, it is probably not prudent.**

INVESTING SMARTLY

Chapter 4

Buying Selectively

Now that you've paid off all the debts you should, reviewed your living costs, and constructed your safety net, you are ready for Step Five: Powerfully creating net worth, financial independence, and security and comfort for your family:

Smart Investing Step Five:

Invest in the excellent wealth-growing engines of equities and real estate, and do so the right way.

The rest of this book is dedicated to discussing exactly how to take Step Five smartly. This and the next two chapters detail exactly what "the right way" means when it comes to ***equity*** investing.

First we'll look at the right way to identify and acquire good equity opportunities (Chapter 4.) Next we'll discuss when it makes sense to sell holdings (Chapter 5.) Finally, we'll enumerate the critical requirements of good portfolio management (Chapter 6.) We will talk about real estate after we are done with equities because many of the important principles of good equity investing are applicable to real estate investing.

You may wonder why we are going to discuss these principles in some detail when we've already established that you are a busy person who just wants to get to it. You might ask, "Isn't there some telephone number I could call to immediately get it done right, so I could skip these chapters?" Sure, you could keep yourself in the dark about these investment principles and perhaps I could give you a number to call to reach someone who could do it for you with expedience (for a fee.) But where will you be if that person moves, or retires, or closes his or her fund to new investment (because so many busy people have called that they became swamped with money)? Then you would be relatively clueless.

I'm sorry, if you want to make sure you do this right – or that you have entrusted your money to someone whom you can be reasonably assured will do it right for you – you have to learn what "the right way" is and develop some appreciation for why it is "right". You don't have to become an expert at putting these principles to work ***yourself***, but you have to be able to identify financial advisers or fund managers who do follow them, rigorously. My goal is to make you very proficient at picking an expert or experts who will do an excellent job on your behalf. That way, when one retires or moves on, you will be capable (perhaps after a brief review of these chapters) of finding someone else to do it just as well.

How Does Owning Equity Grow Your Wealth?

First, let's consider the two ways that a shareholder makes money in equity investing.

1. **Dividends**. Many companies directly pay shareholders a portion of their profits each year in the form of dividends, typically so many cents per share paid quarterly or annually. This is "passive" income as opposed to "active", because you didn't do any work to earn it. That's pretty nice, to be able to make money while you do nothing. Moreover, the IRS presently treats qualified dividends like long-term capital gains, meaning they are taxed at 15% instead of the normally much higher marginal federal income tax rate.

2. **Stock Price Appreciation**. The other way to grow your wealth by owning equities is, of course, price appreciation. As long as you hold a stock, no taxation takes a bite out of its value. If and when you sell your shares in a company, the gain (or loss) is realized and you owe capital gains tax if there is a gain. If you have held the security for at least twelve months, any gain is taxed at the long-term capital gains rate, which again is lower than the federal tax you likely pay on other income.

Typically there is an inverse relation between what a company passes out in dividends each year as a percent of its market price and the stock's appreciation potential. The idea is that slower growing companies have to offer "something" to make up for that problem if they want their shares to be desirable. The "something" is often nice big dividends.

If a company is really going nowhere or contracting, though, it will eventually have to reduce or eliminate its dividend payout. Then what do the shareholders have?

Don't focus on the dividends that a company is paying now, but, rather, the company's future profit potential. If that potential is excellent and you can get the company at a good price, in time appreciation is likely to be good and the company is likely to be able to pay whatever dividend they do offer well into the future.

The best investment opportunities happen when two things are present: a really *good company,* available at a really *good price.* The intelligent goal of equity investing is to become a part-owner of some of the world's best-managed, most-profitable, and well-defended companies, preferably in growing industries, and to buy them when they are selling at bargain prices. These opportunities don't come along everyday. But, when they do, the investor must be able to recognize them and be positioned to take advantage of them.

A Good Company

A truly good company passes the "Rip Van Winkle" test. I think this test was first described by Warren Buffett, who has taught us so much about investing in good companies. The idea is that if you fell asleep for ten years, you could be confident that, when you awoke ten years later, your company would still be a solid profit producer with the same essential qualities you bought it for originally. If so, it's a good company - maybe a great one.

Think of companies like Coca-Cola (KO), Western Union (WU), Johnson and Johnson (JNJ), American Express (AXP). None of these companies has been producing profits for less than 110 years; there is little reason to feel anxious about where they will be ten years from now. This is also true of many younger companies because of their business models. Certainly some companies which would be hard pressed to pass the Rip Van Winkle test may still be good investments, but it's a more "iffy" proposition. Is everyone going to be searching the net using Google in ten years? What if someone outside of Google invents a better search algorithm or people learn a better way to find what they need? How long did it take Google to overtake all contenders as "the" search tool of choice? Don't get me wrong, what Google has accomplished is marvelous, but in ten years, many innovations could affect the profit making potential of Google. If I bought Google today, particularly at a huge price-to-earnings ratio, my ten-year sleep might be a touch anxious.

Since some newer and some older companies can pass the Rip Van Winkle test, you need a set of qualities to look for that can identify good companies of both the young and old variety. Here are the three things you want in a company you acquire:

1. Good "moat" characteristics.
2. Good economics
3. Good management

Let's delve into each one separately.

Good "Moat" Characteristics

The moat of a medieval castle protected it from incursion by its enemies. In a similar fashion, some businesses have "moats" in the form of competitive advantages or unique selling propositions they can offer their customers which competitors, for one reason or another, cannot. These advantages act as a moat that keeps the enemy (the competition) out.

Sometimes these competitive advantages are fleeting and sometimes they are not.

Fleeting Competitive Advantages

If a specialty semiconductor chip manufacturer has the market cornered on a particular type of chip today, that competitive advantage often lasts for a very short time before a newer, better, faster chip is invented. Now the company is in trouble unless it can come up with the next big thing. It must incur high research and development expenses if it hopes to survive the inevitable competition. A billion-dollar plant constructed to make a chip could become obsolete within two or three years. You would think the high cost of the plant development would suggest a big "barrier to entry" for competition, but it has not worked out that way for some semiconductor companies. The real barrier problem is the lack of a moat, or barrier to the competition, for a company whose competitive advantage is fleeting.

Sustainable Competitive Advantages (Moats)

Let's consider an imaginary scenario that will focus you on the power of a truly sustainable competitive advantage. This analogy is another Buffett favorite. Imagine that you own the only bridge to an island. Let's call it Manhattan. Not only do you have the ***only*** bridge, but there are no tunnels. People could take a boat or fly in from the mainland, but if anyone wants to drive over they have to pay to use your bridge. Now that's a distinct competitive advantage.

Let's add that, through some good fortune, the authorities have given you exclusive rights to that bridge and all future bridges and tunnels to Manhattan for 100 years. Now your competitive advantage is ***sustainable***. Not only will everyone driving into Manhattan have to pay you, but if you feel like increasing the toll, you can. A few may accost you with some of those colorful New York City greetings, but most will grudgingly pay the new toll. What's their choice?

What does this do to your profitability? It costs you nothing to raise the price (you didn't have to conduct R&D or build a new bridge). At most you had to put up new signage announcing the new rate. Oh my. Virtually all the additional revenue would fall to the bottom line and your net profit would soar.

That's the ultimate example of the power of sustainable competitive advantages (moats.) Of course, the monopolistic bridge scenario we just described is a fantasy, but some companies enjoy moats almost as powerful.

There are four sources of sustainable competitive advantages, and companies can have a moat based on any one of these or a combination of them. The first two, in my opinion, are the more powerful sources of sustainable competitive advantage. The last two can develop a moat at times, but it is usually not as deep or wide.

The Two More Powerful Moat Characteristics

1. **Intellectual and Intangible Assets.** These assets can come in many forms:

   a. ***Brand names*** can create moats, especially when the products dominate the category. Some brand names are so powerful and ubiquitous that they are virtually synonymous with the product category. I'll order a ginger ale, but I never order a "cola"; I order a "Coke" or "Pepsi." I don't use "facial tissue"; I use "Kleenex". But, of course, it's not Kleenex. Kleenex is a brand name owned by Kimberly Clark (KMB). And the brand name doesn't have to be a verbal substitute for the category to be powerful. What's the #1 laundry detergent? Tide, and look at all the shelf space it gets in the supermarket. The Tide name (just like the Coke name) wins the biggest shelf space, which helps to perpetuate the dominance of the product. And good brand names last and last.

   b. ***Patent Protection*** creates moats, although they don't last forever. Pfizer (PFE) and other pharmaceutical companies enjoy the protection of patent on drugs they invent for many years. They often extend the competitive advantage past the initial term of the patent by patenting modifications and improvements to the drug. Pfizer has the patent on the largest-selling medicine of all time, Lipitor, designed to lower cholesterol in the blood. The $50 billion in Lipitor sales since 2000 has been responsible for a huge share of Pfizer's net profits.

c. ***License Protection*** is another powerful moat builder that can last a long time. International Game Technology (IGT) is the biggest purveyor of gaming ("slot") machines and gaming systems in the world. The slot machine industry is, to say the least, highly regulated. The licensing process is rigorous, so getting into the business is not easy. The result: IGT is, in essence, somewhat isolated from competition. But the company has not been complacent about its competitive advantage. It has worked to bring many innovative machines and systems to market that help their customers (casino owners) become more profitable. The reward has been over a 400% increase in owner's earnings at IGT in the past five years.

d. ***Special Reputation with Key People***. This is that intangible respect for a firm's abilities in a certain area that set it apart. General Dynamics (GD), the defense contractor, enjoys that status with regard to the design and construction of submarines, tanks, and many other complex systems it sells to the military. On a smaller scale, a firm you may never have heard of, Simpson Manufacturing (SSD), designs, engineers and manufactures, among other things, wood-to-wood, wood-to-concrete, and wood-to-masonry connections to strengthen, support, and connect joints in building and fixture construction. They do this through their subsidiary, Simpson Strong-Tie. Simpson Strong

Tie™ connectors absolutely dominate the market for connectors and that dominance has strengthened as housing codes have gotten tougher in the wake of recent hurricanes and earthquakes. Why has Simpson been able to build such dominance when, obviously, anyone could manufacture a connector? The moat is all about the respect the company has earned in the architectural and engineering communities where it has consistently designed and tested connectors that are, simply, superior. As a result, Simpson connectors are the standard specified for most jobs, the way your doctor specifies Lipitor, if your cholesterol is high. I visited a Home Depot store last week and asked the store manager where the other brands of connectors were. He looked as me curiously and said "What other brands?"

2. **The Network Effect.** A few companies are in the enviable position of having a lot of customers...because they have a lot of customers. Perhpas the best-known company that has a huge network effect working for it is eBay (EBAY). People go to eBay to buy and sell things because so many people are there doing the same thing. If you wanted to start a new company to buy/sell/auction items owned by other people, how could you compete with eBay? Who would come to your site if they thought there were very few other people using it? It would take a competitor who already had a lot of people using it (such as Google or Amazon) to even contemplate such a move, and even then it is questionable whether eBay could be unseated in its dominance of the business. That's the power of the network effect. EBay's stock price has gone up about tenfold since it went public in late 1998.

   Another type of company that enjoys this power is the exchanges that handle the trading of futures and options, such as The Chicago Board of Trade (BOT), most famous for agricultural futures, The Chicago Mercantile Exchange (CME), most famous for futures on the US stock indexes and Eurodollar interest rates, and others. People who need to buy and sell futures and options come to these companies to do so because that's where the buyers and seller of the particular futures are. The two "Chicago" firms both became public over the past few years and it took the analysts at the top brokerage houses a long time to appreciate the power of the network effect working for those exchanges. I often find that Wall Street analysts, incidentally, just don't get what is really happening with the companies they follow. Some of them still don't understand it in the case of these two exchanges, but the market has seen their profits soar and has rewarded both of them. The Chicago Mercantile Exchange went public in 2003 and has risen to over tenfold its original price in that short period. The Board of Trade was a later starter (late 2005), but it has already more than doubled in price since then (over that 18 month period.)

The Two Weaker Moat Characteristics

1. **High Switching Costs Relative to Price**. If a product or service is not terribly expensive, the "costs" of switching from it to a competitor may be too high to be worth switching. My oldest son, who is a certified tech and computer genius, is always trying to get me to switch to a different web browser or a different system to get e-mail or some such thing. But, to his chagrin, I am stubbornly resistant because I am familiar with how to work the programs I've got and there is nothing terribly wrong with them. I'm sure I'd gain new features I might learn to like in the new programs, but, to me, it's not worth the hassle

and time it will take to play with my computer to get it right and then learn all about the new platform. The "switching costs" are too high. So, I stick with what I have.

Similarly, Automatic Data Processing (ADP), which is a leader in payroll processing, benefits from the fact that its customers just don't want to be bothered switching, even if something a little better or a little cheaper comes along. As long as the company's services are not a problem, people stick with ADP. The company's customer retention rate is super. This type of moat is not as strong as the first two because if something ***much*** better came along, the complacent masses may be attracted enough to switch. That's exactly what happened when Google spread like wildfire. People discovered it was ***much*** better for finding what they wanted on the Internet fast, without those maddening advertising pop-ups getting in the way, and they moved en masse.

2. **Being the Low Cost Producer.** This is the type of moat I respect the least. It indicates that there is very little difference between the products of one competitor and the next; one company has simply figured out how to make the product (or offer the service) at a considerably lower cost than the others. Sometimes it's difficult for competitors to achieve the same low-cost structure as the leader, as in the case of Wal-Mart's (WMT) competitors. In this case you have a longer-term, but still not terribly powerful, competitive advantage.

   Sometimes competitors, if they are determined and innovative enough, can achieve a cost structure as low as or close to the low cost leader's. Dell Computer (DELL), for example, had a big low-cost advantage coming from 1) lower actual production costs and 2) lower distribution costs due to its direct sales model. In the past two years, Dell's profits and stock price have come under a lot of

> pressure, however, as competitors like Hewlett-Packard have greatly narrowed Dell's cost advantages. What can happen when the low cost provider is no longer clearly lower? The competitors can wind up in price wars that take what is normally a low net margin business even lower. That's not a pretty thing.

One of the great indicators that a company may have powerful "moat" characteristics working for it is its long-term history of return on invested capital and/or return on assets. A good investment manager will study these indicators carefully when hunting for good moat companies or when testing the hypothesis that a moat exists at a company. A long history of high returns on invested capital almost invariably indicates some kind of a moat.

In summary, you want to buy companies that have disciplined plans for good long-term growth, and also have inherent "moats", or sustainable competitive advantages, that make it difficult or impossible for new or old competitors to share in that growth or compromise the firm's ability to price its products and services to achieve strong profits on the capital invested in the business.

Good Economics

To understand how good a company's economics are, you - or the person with whom you have entrusted your money - must study the financial statements of the company. I like to be able to look at ten years of financial statements so that I can get a clear picture of trends and past problems. We won't get into all that's involved with reading and interpreting financial statements here, but it is important to understand what separates the good companies from the not-so-good when looking at the statements. There are three key factors of a company's economics, really:

1. **Profitability.** How good the company has been at producing profits is, admittedly, a look in the rear-view mirror. If you have already determined that a company has sustainable competitive advantages, the past is often a decent indicator of what you can expect in the future. This depends, though, on how sustainable that competitive advantage is. I study three items to identify profit machines:

   a. The company's ten-year history of return on invested capital. The company's return on invested capital should be in excess of its cost of capital. This demonstrates wise capital investment by the management, and that the business is in sound shape. The higher the return on invested capital the better.

   b. The company's ten-year history of owner's earnings. This requires a little accounting understanding, but it's worth it. Most analysts focus on net income and hang on every quarter's changes in net income. But net income is a number that can be manipulated by a company pretty easily (not that any of them would ever do that, right?) Let's say a company's management achieves a growth in net income from one year to the next of $100 million. Sounds good... particularly if it represents, say, a 15% growth in profits. But what if they had to spend an additional $100 million a year in capital expenditures to achieve and maintain that increase in net profits? If you owned 100% of that company, would you get any increase in the income you could take home (the owner's earnings) based on that $100 million boost in net income? No...not a penny. So don't let net income fool you. Owner's earnings are calculated by taking net income for the year, subtracting capital expenditures for that year and subtracting any increase in working capital, then adding back the amounts noted in the income statement for depreciation and amortization (because these are non-cash expenses.)

I'll use the 2006 financials of Coca- Cola to demonstrate:

Coca-Cola (KO)2006	Amount in $ Billions
Net Income:	5.080
Less Capital Expenditures:	- 1.407
	3.673
Less Increase in Working Capital:	- .615
	3.058
Add Back Non-Cash Items:	
Depreciation/Amortization:	+ .938
Owner's Earnings:	3.996

Now you know what a 100% owner of the business could have taken home at the end of 2006. By looking at a ten-year history of owner's earnings, you learn a lot about the ***real*** profitability of the business and where it is headed.

c. The third thing I like to get an idea about is how big a profit-margin business this is and if its profits are getting squeezed or expanding. Looking at a ten year history, once again, is helpful. I always prefer a business that has nice fat gross-profit margins and net-profit margins. Fat or thin, gross-profit margins that are headed downward are often a sign that competition is starting to heat up and squeeze a firm's ability to charge decent prices. That can spell trouble. On the other hand, I love it when I see net profit margins expanding over the past ten years. ***That*** business is becoming a stronger and stronger profit engine.

2. **Financial strength.** Here, you're looking for a reasonably low debt-to-equity ratio. Some companies have no debt at all and others are leveraged to the hilt (i.e., they have huge long-term debt to pay interest on yearly). In tough economic times, companies with heavy debt can become pressured. If you owned a business that had significant debt during the 1970s or early 80s (when interest rates soared) you have, as I do, a particularly well-developed appreciation for the onerous effects of debt and its attendant debt service. Heavily leveraged companies can go bankrupt in tough times, leaving stockholders with shares of little or no value. You want to see no debt or a reasonably low debt level relative to cash flow from operations, making it an amount of debt that the company can easily service.

3. **A History of Relatively Low Capital Expenditure.** There are companies that produce good profits every year, but need to replace plant and equipment at a rate that eats up much of that profit with capital expenditures. The airline industry has this problem because planes are expensive. Look at American Airlines' parent company, AMR Corporation (AMR). Over the past eleven years (1996-2006) AMR spent an average of 115% of its cash flow from operations on capital expenditures each year. It spent an amount not only equal to all of its cash flow from operations every year, but 15% more! This partially explains why AMR has a market capitalization (arrived at by multiplying the number of shares outstanding times the price per share) of about $7 billion, while it carries total long term debt of over $12 billion. Amazing.

Good Management

So far we've covered "moat" characteristics and economics. I saved the evaluation of management for last—on purpose.

Peter Lynch said it best in *One Up On Wall Street*: "Go for a business that any idiot could run – because sooner or later any idiot is probably going to run it." If you have a business with a great moat and solid economics, all will be well in the long run, even if you are asleep for ten years like Rip Van Winkle. In fact, it is better that you have a nice long sleep and ignore what the idiot does with the business until he or she is eventually canned.

Warren Buffet pointed out that when a ***good*** manager does his or her best to turnaround a ***bad*** business, it is the reputation of the latter that usually survives. Good managers can certainly turn around strong businesses that have been mismanaged, but if the business is truly "bad", in the sense that it lacks sustainable competitive advantages or good economics, that's far less likely.

Management can only do so much—good or bad. It's kind of like the President of the United States. The United States is, basically, very sound, so it prospers through good and bad presidents. If a company has sustainable competitive advantages and sound economics, it will do well, too. So it's smart to study those things first.

That said, there are three things about the management of a company that are valuable to understand, so let's review them.

1. **Are the Top Managers Investor-Minded?** Do they have enough ownership of the company to be co-motivated with shareholders to produce profits that will cause the stock to appreciate? The larger the percentage of the company that is owned by top management, the better.

   The opposite of the investor-minded manager is the "professional manager" who doesn't own much of the company and isn't remunerated based on measures that are aligned with the interests of the shareholders, such as growth in owner's earnings or return on invested capital. This type of manager may only care about making sure his or her own nest is well-feathered.

2. **Is the CEO Good at Allocating Capital?** This is really the most important job of the top person at a company. Great managers allocate capital in ways that yield improved profit. If there is nothing to do that will increase profitability, they return the excess capital to the shareholders in the form of either increased dividends or share buy-backs when their stock is favorably priced. The ability to wisely allocate capital shows up, once again, in the company's history of return on invested capital. The opposite would be the manager who is an empire builder, squandering resources on a fancy corporate office or fleet of jets that might be impressive to the CEO's "friends", but yield no increase in profitability.

3. **Are the Top Managers Candid About Their Mistakes and Challenges?** You can listen to their conference calls on-line these days and, if you are a shareholder of a company, you can go to their annual shareholder's meeting. You can also read what they have to say in the "Management Discussion" section of their earnings reports. Listening to what key managers have to say and how they say it helps you understand whether they are a bunch of windbags who never admit when they've screwed up (and everybody screws up occasionally) or whether they are in touch with reality and are hard at work fixing problems they have identified.

Your Shopping List

If you find that a company has a good moat, good economics and good management, you have a good company - one you would like to buy at the right price. At the wrong price, a good company does not constitute a good investment. It would, however, make it to your "shopping list" where you would include it with other companies you'd like to own at the right price.

So that I can jump on one of these good companies when their price gets low enough to represent a good deal, I keep a shopping list of companies I like, along with the price at which I would be willing to consider buying them. Through the miracle of the Internet, the actual stock price of every company on the list is updated every thirty seconds or so. When the price of a company's stock gets down to a price at which I would ***consider*** buying it, an audible alarm goes off in my office and I go to work investigating why its price has come down.

I may feel, after studying the situation, that there is no good reason for the price to have declined. The reason it has dipped may be something that people shouldn't be concerned about (an overblown fear or a rumor) or something that will only depress the company's profits temporarily and then disappear. If so, then I may move to acquire the stock.

We'll discuss the calculation of what constitutes a "good price" in a moment, but first, you may be asking yourself how one finds these good companies. How do good investment managers develop a wonderful shopping list?

Many use a variety of automatic screening programs that identify companies which possess certain characteristics, such as a low price-to-earnings ratio, to initially get companies "on the radar", so to speak. But the best sources of companies that actually wind up in a successful portfolio, in my experience, are not these screeners.

Four sources consistently yield the finest ideas:

1. By reading of all types of publications. When the company's economics are right, reading can help one learn, in depth, about the continued economic prospects of the firm and the industry it is in. Leads that come from reading something meaningful about the company and why it might be solid in its prospects (and, better still, undervalued!) are more to my liking than a company just "popping up" on a screener.

2. By attending certain investment conferences which mention companies worth looking at and why they might be worthy of consideration. While he was alive, the Louis Rukeyser conventions occasionally contained gems of wisdom that were helpful. A relative newcomer in the world of conferences that I've come to like is Whitney Tilson's Value Investing Congress. It features some of the best value investors in America sharing their most promising ideas (www.valueinvestingcongress.com.)

3. By talking with industry insiders—people who observe companies in an industry while working within it.

4. By talking with ***outside*** experts, who really understand an industry and the businesses within it at a deep level, but don't actually work in the industry at present.

The latter source is, I should emphasize, not a Wall Street analyst. Wall Street analysts usually work for firms that want or already have relationships with companies they follow. They are potentially hampered by conflicts of interest and are not always aware of what is happening in companies they follow that could affect future profit growth or reduction. I generally pay little attention to what Wall Street analysts say. I am more interested in the opinions of smart people who have deep knowledge of particular industries and have nothing to gain from me buying or not buying a company's stock.

I know you don't have time to do all this searching and analysis yourself, but being aware of these concepts will benefit you greatly when you are ready to interview a manager you are considering or review the strategy description of a fund. Remember, no matter how good a fund's return has been, you are not buying its past return. That return went to the people who invested in the fund in the past. When you buy into a fund or hire a money manager, what you are really getting for your money are the principles used by the fund to achieve its results and a fund manager you anticipate will practice those principles going forward. What I'm passing along to you are methods to evaluate both.

A Good Price

Morningstar, Inc., a leading provider of independent investment research with coverage of more than 1900 stocks and over 2000 mutual funds, publishes a monthly newsletter for individual investors called *Morningstar StockInvestor*. In the September 2005 issue of *Morningstar StockInvestor,* Editor Paul Larson wrote the article *The Importance of Buying Cheaply,* which contains perhaps the best argument I have ever read for the importance of buying stocks only when they are available at good prices:

> *If you had invested equal amounts in the following companies five years ago, how do you think your investments would have fared?*

Coca-Cola	*(KO)*
Dell	*(DELL)*
General Electric	*(GE)*
Microsoft	*(MSFT)*
Wal-Mart	*(WMT)*

> *Pretty impressive group of companies, no? In your portfolio you would have had a company with one of the best brands in the world, a dominant and fast-growing computer company, the world's most successful industrial company, a near-monopolistic software titan, and a behemoth of a retailer. All are bellwethers that have major advantages against their competitors, and all produce handsome cash flows and returns on capital …*
>
> *Unfortunately, for those who bought this group of companies five years ago, the dream team has been a set of big losers from an investment perspective. As a group, they are down approximately 15% on average. Instead of being an owner in these stalwarts of American business, you would have been better off stuffing the cash in a mattress or (gasp!) in a savings account with a 0.5% interest rate.*

A good company can be a bad investment. It always amazes me how many investors and fund managers fail to understand the importance of only buying good companies when they are available at a very good price. You would think everybody would get it immediately, but, I promise you, they don't. This basic idea is the backbone of "value investing," and this book certainly espouses a particular and specific approach to value investing.

Is this idea really the backbone solely of "value investing", though, or is it the backbone of *all* intelligent investing? The "fair value" or "intrinsic value" of a company is the real value that a knowledgeable buyer of 100% of a company would be willing to pay for it, based on its long-term profit prospects. If a fund manager or investor is not focused on buying good companies only when they are at least at - and preferably well below - their fair value, how could you call that investing? Paying over the fair value of a company is really speculating. You are, in essence, gambling that some greater fool in the future will be willing to pay even more.

There are two critical advantages to refusing to buy good companies unless their price on the open market is substantially below their fair value: more return and more safety. Let's examine each.

More Return

Imagine for a moment that you believe the fair value of a good company you have been studying is $50. I don't want to get technical here, but there are a number of ways to get a reasonable idea of the fair value of a company. What works best for me is a version of the "discounted cash flow model," which focuses on owner's earnings. I project into the future the owner's earnings for the company and then discount the sum of all these future values to account for the time value of money. The time value of money takes into account the fact that a dollar ten years from now is worth a lot less than a dollar today due to the devaluing effects of inflation.

Here's a demonstration of what the calculation of fair value of a company looks like using this discounted cash flow method. If you're not interested, feel free to skip ahead.

For this example, I'm going to show you the calculation of the fair value of the Chicago Mercantile Exchange I did in 2003 that led me to make that purchase. Let's do this is a series of steps:

1. First, calculate the last year of owner's earnings for The Merc to develop a starting point:

Actual reported 2002 Net Income:	94,070,000	
Less Capital Expenditures	-37,293,333	
Less Increase in Working Capital	(1,780,000)	since WC decreased
	58,556,667	
Add back non-cash expenses of		
Depreciation and Amortization:	+39,880,000	
2002 Owner's Earnings:	98,436,667	

2. Next, assume a growth rate for the first stage of the company's growth, usually the first 10 years, project out the rising owner's earnings, and then discount back each year to get a present value for each and add all those present values together. I assumed 10% growth per year (which turned out to be quite conservative) and used a 7% discount rate at that time. Using the standard way to calculate present value of a future sum (so that the discount factor is 1/((1+discount rate expressed in hundredths) to the *n*th power), where *n* is the year number, the calculations look like this: (Figures given as thousands)

Year	Prior Yr OE	Growth	Yr's OE	Discount factor	Discounted Value
1	98,436	10%	108,280	1.9346	101,196
2	108,280	10%	119,106	.8734	104,033
3	119,106	10%	131,019	.8163	106,950
4	131,019	10%	144,121	.7629	109,949
5	144,121	10%	158,533	.7130	113,032
6	158,533	10%	174,386	.6663	116,201
7	174,386	10%	191,825	.6227	119.495
8	191,825	10%	211,007	.5820	122,808
9	211,007	10%	232,108	.5439	126,251
10	232,251	10%	255,319	.5083	129,791
	Total of Present Value of Cash Flows for 10 years				1,149,674

That gives us the present value of all the owner's earnings for the first 10 years – the stage one growth years – of the business. But there's more value to this business at the end of the ten years, of course. An estimate of this residual value has to be added to the above figure.

3. I assumed that the stage 2 growth rate – for years #11 and thereafter – would be only 3% (again, a conservative estimate). The owner's earnings for Year #11 would be 255,319 grown by 3%, or 262,978. To discount the owner's earnings going forward, divide this amount by the capitalization rate, which is the discount rate (of 7%) less the assumed growth rate (of 3%), or 4%:

   $$262{,}978/.04 = 6{,}574{,}450$$

   To get the present value of the residual at the end of year ten, then, take 6,570,450 times the discount factor for year ten (.5083) . That gives us 3,342,128.

4. So, the total present value of the company would be the present value of the owner's earnings flow for the first ten years of the company's growth (1,149,674) plus the present value of the residual of the company's life going forward (3,342,128), or a total of 4,491,803. That's about $4.5 billion; keep in mind, because the figures we were using were expressed as thousands.

5. To get the present value **per share**, divide this sum of $4,491,803,000 by the number of shares outstanding, which at that time was 32,530,000. This yields a fair value estimate of $138.08 per share. At the time I did this analysis, shares of the company were selling for under $70, about a 50% discount to its fair value.

There are other methods that can be used to estimate fair value; the critical thing is for the investor or portfolio manager to get to a good guess for a firm's fair value, regardless of the method used.

Now, let's assume that my best guess is that the fair value of each share of a company I am studying is $50. Further, I believe the fair value of the company will grow 10% per year over the next five years. Therefore I am projecting, as best I can, that the fair value of the company at the end of five years will be $80.52 - that's $50 growing at 10% for five years.

Now, assuming that that's exactly what happens and that five years from now the company's stock is actually selling for $80.52. Let's look at the difference in investment returns depending upon the purchase price.

If you purchased this stock at $75, you would have made money. You would have made the difference between $75 and $80.52, so that's $5.52, or a 7.36% growth in your investment over the five years. Not so great.

Had you paid $50 (the full fair value you calculated) for the company, you would have made the difference between $50 and $80.52 or $30.52, or 61.04% growth in five years. That's certainly better.

What if you waited to buy it one day at $25...a 50% discount to its fair value? You would make the difference, in this case, between $25 and $80.52, or $55.52, or a 222% increase in your investment. Now we're talking!

The difference between making a huge return on this company's stock and just "OK" returns was waiting for a very low price - waiting until the market was, in essence, offering one dollar for 50 cents, and then moving to buy it. "50-cent dollars" happen when the company, or the industry the company's in, is out of favor. Market conditions may not be favorable or the market may be running scared and does not properly perceive the true long-term value of the company.

"50-cent dollars" are all I care to buy. I refuse to buy a good company's stock until I believe it is selling for 50% or less of its fair value. Some good investors will buy at 55%, or 60%, or even 70% of what they have estimated fair value to be. Different people approach it differently. But all good investors, in my opinion, wait for a significant discount to the real or fair value before buying.

Well, you might say, those probably don't come along very often, do they? True, but how many do you need? You do need some diversity in your stock portfolio (we'll cover that in Chapter 7), but if all you buy is "50-cent dollars", you don't need a lot of opportunities to do well, do you? If all you bought was the one company I described above and held it for five years, your average annual return would have been pretty fantastic.

Smart investors wait patiently for just the fat pitches before they swing - good companies at great prices. Are you in a fund that holds stocks of 50 or 100 or 150 companies? Most mutual funds have a portfolio containing that many names. Nobody is patiently waiting for the fat pitch in these funds. They are too busy swinging. As Warren Buffett counseled, "The stock market is a no-strikes-called game. You don't have to swing at everything – you can wait for your pitch."

More Safety

Truthfully, when a fund manager – even a smart, well-informed manager – estimates the fair value of a company, he or she is just estimating. And the estimate can easily be wrong. In the example we gave above, let's say that my estimate of fair value was wrong and that I had overestimated what it was worth. Clearly, if I had, ***underestimated*** it, all the buyers I described above would just have realized a more impressive gain. But assume I ***overestimated*** it. Instead of being worth $50 and growing at 10% per year, let's say the real value of the company was more like $40 and it grew at 5% per year, and at the end of year five, its full value was reflected in its price, so that it was priced at $51. Now, how did our three different buyers do?

The person who originally paid $75 for the stock lost $24, or 32% of his or her investment. The investor who paid $50, made $1, or about 2% over the five years. The value investor who paid $25 for it made $26, or 105% over the five years. Even when the original estimate of fair value was, in retrospect, too optimistic, this value buyer still did pretty well.

Now you see the increased safety that buying only at good low prices brings. Smart investors focus on the downside risk of a potential acquisition as much as they do the upside potential, but they can and do still make mistakes about the actual prospects of a firm and, thus, it's real fair value. If they are selective enough only to buy when the stock appears to be ***way*** undervalued, they enjoy what Ben Graham, the father of value investing, called the "margin of safety." Graham wrote, "The margin of safety in the central concept of investment."

Another way that buying good companies at cheap prices increases your safety is that it makes your investment portfolio somewhat insulated from general market downturns. You are not reliant on the value of the overall market to create your return. There are even times when the market's decline can push the prices of good undervalued companies ***up*** substantially. I recall buying shares of Washington Mutual (WM) in early 2000, when those shares had been beaten down to a split-adjusted price of about $14. Now, 2000 was when the market started falling. Money started getting out of tech and Internet stocks in a big way. Where did the money go? Well, enough of it went to Washington Mutual stock that its price nearly tripled in just over a year.

A Better Price

Often a value investor buys shares of a company at a good price and the price of these shares goes down. In 2000, I bought Abercrombie and Fitch (ANF), the hip youth apparel company, when its shares had fallen from $50 to $18 over the previous 12 or 13 months. I did not think ANF shares were worth $50 at that moment, but I believed that they were worth at least $36, so I purchased the stock. I thought it was a good, if not great, company. It had some moat in its brand, pretty good economics, and very good top management.

What happened? Its share price fell further, within a fairly short period, to $13, and I bought some more. Mind you, I had to search my soul to be very sure my estimate of fair value was not terribly off base, but now I only had to believe the shares were worth at least $26 to make it a great deal, and I still felt quite sure about the $36 fair value.

What happened then? The share price fell to $8.00. That's a scary moment. You wonder what you could possibly be missing. With somewhat sweaty palms, you run the numbers and review the facts all over again. I did and I still felt very sure that my original estimate of fair value was correct, so I backed up the truck and bought a lot. In roughly one year the share price rose to about $47.

Such precipitous and continued drops are not an uncommon phenomenon when one spots a stock selling for way less than its worth. Its price is, in essence, de-coupled from its real value.

Institutes of higher learning often teach something in their investment courses called "The Efficient Market Theory". The central premise of this theory, posited by University of Chicago professor Eugene Fama, is that the market is so efficient that all that is known about a company and its future prospects is fully reflected in its price at any moment. According to the Theory, this, in turn, means that the actual market price at any moment will be a "good estimate" of its fair value. Clearly, given the

Abercrombie and Fitch example, this is not the case, is it? Short term pricing mistakes by the market – both undervaluation and overvaluation – are made every day.

When the market makes a mistake, as it did in the case of Abercrombie, sellers sometimes can't dump the stock fast enough. The price, de-coupled from its real value, can fall to ridiculously low valuations. It's not always easy to double down during such fear-ridden times, but it is what the best value investors do. The nice thing is, the lower it goes, the safer is your entire investment in the company, as you average down the price at which you are invested. With these kinds of cascading price drops, if you're buying on the way down you can still turn out just fine, even if you were originally somewhat too optimistic about the company's fair value.

Key Take-Away Points from Chapter 4

- **The intelligent goal of investing is to become a part-owner of a select group of the world's best companies and to do so when they are available at a price significantly below their fair value.**

- **Three things are most indicative of a firm's value and future prospects:**

  1. **Excellent "moat" characteristics – particularly *sustainable* competitive advantages.**

  2. **Advantageous economics – good profitability in terms of return on invested capital, financial strength (low debt-to-equity ratio), and lack of a need for high annual capital expenditures to maintain profitable growth.**

3. Top management that is co-motivated with the shareholders, is prudent in allocating the firm's capital, and is realistic and humble enough to realize and admit mistakes and problems and address them.

- The essence of value investing is purchasing the shares of such exceptional companies only when there is enough of a "margin of safety" so that the price of the shares represents a sizable discount to their fair value – fair value being calculated by the discounted value of future cash flows or some other dependable method.

Chapter 5

Selling Smartly

Having a Compass: Fair Value

What did I do when the price of the Abercrombie and Fitch stock rose to about $47? I sold it. Actually I sold it a bit before it got to $47. A lot of people sell stocks because they feel it's wise to "take your gains." Clearly there had been a huge gain in the stock in a short period of time, but that's not why I sold. Why did I sell?

The method of buying good companies at good prices I discussed in the last chapter makes it unnecessary to sell very often because, if you follow those precepts, you will wind up owning a group of very fine companies that create additional shareholder value year after year. As a result, their fair value keeps rising year after year. If an investor or fund manager does not recalculate the company's fair value annually (or whenever he or she is tempted by a high price to sell), how do they possibly know when it is wise or unwise to sell? Not developing a new estimate of fair value for each of the companies you own, on a regular basis, leaves you without a compass. You simply don't know when to sell; at least you don't know when it makes good sense to do so.

I believe many managers and investors just guess when to sell. They see the stock price grow in a certain company and they move to take gains, without rigorously calculating what the stock ***should*** be priced at, considering its profit prospects.

I sold the Abercrombie and Fitch stock when I did because its price had risen above what I estimated its fair value to be at the moment, taking everything into account I knew about the business and its future prospects. If that had not been the case – if the fair value of the company had ratcheted up to, say, $75 or $100 – I would have been silly to sell. The price of Abercrombie and Fitch stock today is, in fact, just over $75, so maybe I was too conservative in the assumed growth rates I used in my calculation of a fair value estimate (and maybe I wasn't), but I was making prudent decisions because they were based upon a rigorously estimated fair value number each time.

I make an updated estimate of a company's fair value yearly and, in addition to that, at any point in time when its actual market price has hit what I had previously calculated to be its full fair value. That's the key. This estimating activity is never a perfect science, of course, but, without a ***reasonably*** accurate compass, an investor can't know when to sell, hold or buy.

One more thing happens with investors who don't have a compass. Their lack of clear direction can cause them to be ravaged by irrational waves of fear and greed that periodically sweep the market. This leads to bad, emotion-prompted decisions, particularly on the selling end of things.

Let me return to the example of the Chicago Mercantile Exchange and its ascending share price that I described briefly in the introduction of this book. I initially bought into the company in 2003 when the stock was priced at about $67. I had estimated a fair value for the company of $138 and I thought it was a good company with some of the best natural economics I'd ever seen. So, since it was priced at about 50% of its fair value, I bought it, and I bought a lot of it. When its price reached $138 I studied it again. This time the company had introduced a lot of new products and raised its volume of transactions and profitability so much that I estimated its fair value had grown to about $210, so I didn't sell.

Admittedly, it wasn't a "50-cent dollar" at that moment. If my calculations were correct, it was about "65-cent dollar." That's not a terrible thing to hold onto once you own it. The same kind of analysis took place when its price reached $200, and $300, etc. I decided to forgo selling it along the way because the fair value was always pushing ahead of the price. So why sell? A lot of people did sell because, I imagine, they lacked the compass of a well-developed estimate of the firm's fair value. We finally sold the last of our shares of the Chicago Mercantile Exchange at $375, and I'm glad I did, even though the price of the stock is now $530. Let's think about why I'm glad.

Selling the Wine Before its Time

Do you remember the advertisement delivered by a bearded Orson Welles for Paul Mason that used to say that the winery would "sell no wine before its time?" Well, you don't want to sell shares in good companies too early, before they have reached their full fair value. And some of the very best companies you own – the ones with excellent moats, great economics, and growing profit potential - may never get to that point. Their stock price grows and grows, but their fair value grows even more, so you hold.

But there are rare occasions when selling a stock ***a bit*** before its time may make sense. As I mentioned, I sold the last of the Merc shares at $375, but I actually had sold some of the shares at an even lower price before that. Based upon the estimate of fair value at that time – the fall of 2003 – the shares were worth around $400. That meant that the shares represented, if you will, "85- to 90-cent dollars." I'm happy to wait, normally, until they grow to "100-cent dollars" before selling, but, at that time, a new opportunity came along that I felt was clearly a 50-cent dollar and it was in the same industry...an industry I understood pretty well by then. It was The Chicago Board of Trade. I opted to sell stock of The Merc and use all the proceeds from those sales, and a good bit more, to buy the Board of Trade. What has been the result? During the period from fall 2003 to today (May 18, 2007) the Merc's price has increased from about $350 to $524.80, a 50% increase. But the Board of Trade's price has increased from $85 to $195.02, a 129% increase.

As I write this, the Chicago Mercantile Exchange is seeking to acquire the Chicago Board of Trade. If it happened, the resulting merged company would be an extreme economic powerhouse.

Smart Selling Guidelines

Smart value investors and value fund managers try not to sell a company until its price has gone beyond their calculation of the stock's fair value. Even then, they do so grudgingly, because it's a good company they are parting with, and good companies don't come along at bargain prices every day.

Here is a set of simple selling guidelines that makes sense:

1. If you are tempted to sell a company, but the fundamentals of that business still look good and the fair value has not yet been reached, don't consider selling unless you have a "special situation" available to you:

"Special Situation" Requirements

a. The stock of the company you are considering ***selling*** is very close to (say, within 20% of) its full fair value, ***and...***

b. The stock of the company you are considering ***buying*** is selling at least 50% below its fair value, and you know and understand the company and industry very well. These special situations often occur with two companies in the same industry, as in the example of selling the Chicago Mercantile Exchange to buy the Chicago Board of Trade.

2. If you are tempted to sell a company and it has reached 100% of what you estimate its fair value to be, first think carefully about whether the company has the ability to ratchet up its profitability rapidly and without a lot of capital infusion. There are very few companies that can but, if they do, the fair value that you estimate today could be outdated (and too low) tomorrow. If the company can't ratchet up profitability easily, you should sell.

3. If a company that has reached your calculation of its full fair value ***does*** have the ability to ratchet up fair value and perhaps has specific plans to do so, it may be wise, in the long-run, to hold. Holding, at least until the price gets so great that the implied multiple of earnings seems indefensible, is usually prudent with these rare gems.

When Holding Does Not Make Sense

Clearly, smart investors should be in no particular hurry to sell their holdings. For many years Warren Buffett swore he would ***never*** sell certain of the core holdings in Berkshire's portfolio, no matter what their price. When I first read this, I knew I'd found the one point, perhaps, on which the master and I strongly disagreed. And nothing since has changed my mind. Why?

Let's say you are holding in your portfolio of good companies one which, due to the capricious whims of the market, has had its price run north of its fair value. Let's also say that although the company has a wonderful moat, good economics and good management, it does not really have an ability to ratchet up profitability easily. There is not a way that it can cheaply develop more profit growth, in the way, for example, that the Chicago Mercantile Exchange did by offering new products at little additional cost to the organization. In this instance, I would say it would be unwise not to sell. Why?

Not selling an overvalued stock from your portfolio is about the same thing as ***buying*** that company's stock when it is overvalued. You are deciding, in essence, to own the stock of a company that is overvalued. If you would not do that on the "buy" side because it doesn't make sense, why does it make sense on the "sell" side?

Since he first made those "hold forever" pledges many years ago, I think even Mr. Buffett has come to rethink this point. I understand it bothered him not to have taken advantage of the irrationally high pricing of Coca-Cola in 1998. In that year, Coke's price soared to almost $90. Today it sells for about $48. That's certainly nearer its fair value.

That's a $42 drop down to some more reasonable reality. Since Berkshire owns 200 million shares of Coca Cola, that's an $8.4 billion dollar difference. It would have been prudent to at least consider selling it at $90, wouldn't it? When the price of one of your holdings goes past what you believe to be its fair value, you should seriously, if grudgingly, consider selling.

If Things Go Bad

The other time to consider selling a holding is if there are fundamental changes within a company - especially in the size or sustainability of its "moat" or its economics - that can negatively impact its long-term ability to generate growing profit and cash flow. Or if you find good solid reason to distrust the management. At a time like this, it doesn't really matter whether you have made or lost money on the holding. If you believe your essential investment thesis doesn't hold water anymore and that the fair value for the troubled company is now below its price (no matter how low that is), my best advice is to cut bait. It's a hard thing to do at the time, because it is an admission of failure in some sense (maybe not yours, but the management's), but it will save you a lot in the long run. A company you bought for $50 which has slid to $40 can represent a much bigger loss if it continues to fall to $30 or $25.

Key Take-Away Points from Chapter 5

- **Unless things have gone bad in one of your holdings– there has been some fundamental negative change in the "moat," economics or management, for example – these are selling guidelines that make good sense:**

  1. **If the price of a holding has not yet reached its full fair value, don't consider selling unless a "special situation" becomes available and the shares you are considering selling are within 20% of fair value.**

  2. **If the price of a holding has reached its full fair value (one you have calculated at that moment), determine whether the company is one that can fairly easily ratchet up its profitability further without large capital infusion. If not, sell.**

3. If the price of a holding has reached its full fair value but it does have the ability to ratchet up profitability easily, it is probably prudent to hold, at least until its price has been bid up to a multiple of earnings which seems indefensible.

Chapter 6

High-Return Portfolio Management

So far we have discussed ***what*** to do if you want to achieve excellent long-term wealth growth using stock investment: buying good companies at favorable prices and selling them when they become overvalued. In this chapter we'll discuss ***how*** to manage the portfolio of stocks to achieve high returns and ***who*** should do it. First, let's discuss "how."

The Principle of Concentration

The late Peter Drucker, one of the most insightful business minds of our age, was not a man who indulged in hyperbole, nor did he use language arbitrarily. So in the following statement – maybe the most important of his career – we have something rather monumental to think about. He said, "Concentration is the key to all economic success."

Notice that he did not say concentration is ***one of the keys*** to all economic success. He did not say concentration was the key to ***some forms*** of economic success. He said it is the key to ***all*** economic success. Clearly, what you are trying to do in building your wealth is an attempt to achieve one form of economic success – perhaps the most important one to you personally. So how are Drucker's words applicable to this effort? If the "margin of safety" idea (only buying good companies when their price is substantially below the fair value of the company) and the need for a good "moat"(strong and sustainable competitive advantages) are two of the three most important ideas in investing, ***concentration*** constitutes the third. And, of the three, I would put it at the very top.

Charlie Munger has been Warren Buffett's investment partner for what seems like forever. Although Charlie is over eighty years old, his mind is sharp as a tack and his investment prowess and knowledge of the world are unequalled. In the Year End 2003 *Outstanding Investor Digest*, Charlie speaks to concentration in equity investing. He addresses whether an investor should feel threatened or poor if they had their investment dollars ***very*** concentrated, specifically in just three entities:

> *Suppose you were a real estate investor with a third interest in by far the best shopping center in town, a third interest in the best office building, and a third interest in some huge apartment complex which was in the right place and managed by wonderful people. Would you feel like a poor threatened real estate investor? The answer is no, you wouldn't.*
>
> *But the minute you get into securities, they try and make you feel* **inadequate** *if you don't have 100 names – some of which you can't even pronounce."*

Munger is suggesting that you would be far better off with a small number of holdings than with 100. But is he really suggesting you should be happy holding just three companies' stocks? Does that seem a little too concentrated to you? I would agree that three stocks is very concentrated and that you do need diversity in your portfolio to help keep you safe if a particular company or a specific industry or sector gets out of favor with the market for an extended period of time.

But what if you owned just ten companies, all in very different sectors of the economy? Then you would have a ***concentrated*** portfolio, because it would not have the 50 to 150 names that your broker or a mutual fund might cause you to own, but it would also be ***diversified.*** You would not have all your eggs in one basket (one industry or sector.) Let's call this a "concentrated but diverse" portfolio. The two key words there are not mutually exclusive. You do not need 100 companies to be adequately diversified, particularly if you are a long-term investor.

Most investors understand the need for diversification, but most don't fully appreciate the power of concentration and, as a result, own too many stocks.

The Power of the "Concentrated but Diverse" Portfolio

If your ownership in equities is concentrated in fewer than twenty companies, it is considered a "focused portfolio." There are five reasons to be focused or concentrated in your investing:

1. **Not All Investment Ideas are Great**. When you focus on just the very best investment opportunities, instead of owning the best ***and*** the "not quite as good" opportunities, it stands to reason that you'll do better. By "very best opportunities" I mean stocks of companies that are excellent businesses ***and*** are trading way below their full fair value. Let's call these your "A" investment ideas. You've learned that "A" ideas aren't easy to find. They don't come along every day. As a result, a portfolio of 100

companies might include a few "A" quality ideas, but must necessarily include many that are "B" (good companies, but not all that undervalued) and probably plenty of "C" ideas (hopefully good companies, but ones which are fully- or over-valued.)

On the other hand, if you hold just ten or so companies in your portfolio that you know very well, your odds of increasing the percentage of "A" investment ideas, and weeding out the "Bs" and "Cs" increases dramatically. Philip Fisher, author of the investment bible *Common Stocks and Uncommon Profits*, noted in his later book *Development of an Investment Philosophy* that "Holding over twenty different stocks is a sign of financial incompetence. Ten to twelve is usually a better number." Gerald M. Loeb, in his classic *The Battle for Investment Survival* opined, "Diversification is an admission of not knowing what to do, and an effort to strike an average."

I believe diversification within a portfolio of ten to twenty stocks is important, but with 100 stocks in your portfolio, your performance doesn't have a chance to excel because all those "B" and "C" holdings will neutralize the success of the "A" investments. If you put 1% of your equity capital into each of 100 companies and the stock of one company doubles, it only drives the portfolio ahead by 1%. If you own 10% of that same company, the effect on the portfolio is huge.

2. **Focus Just Seems to Work.** Empirically, the evidence is clear that concentrated portfolios work. Warren Buffet enjoyed some of his most stellar returns when he owned just three companies. Loads of the most successful investors in history – Warren and Charlie of Berkshire Hathaway; the late Bill Ruane of the Sequoia Fund; Lou Simpson, CEO of Geico Insurance (who normally has about ten stocks in Geico's portfolio); John Maynard Keynes of the

Chest Fund; and Bill Nygren in his Oakmark Select Fund have all run focused portfolios. Over the long haul, they have all managed to beat the market not by a point or two, but by eight or more percentage points.

3. **Lack of Focus Seems to Fail.** Empirically, the evidence suggests widely diversified portfolios don't usually do well. The more stocks you have in a portfolio, the more you mirror the market. Once you hold more than thirty companies, it gets harder and harder, mathematically, to beat the indices. A portfolio with 100 stocks in it is, in effect, its own index. The average mutual fund these days holds about 100 names (and may have 80% or more turnover each year!). Although they may enjoy a good year or a short run of good years relative to the market, the great majority of mutual funds don't excel in the long run. A study done in the late 90s, for example, found that, in the twenty-year period between 1977 and 1997, a whopping 75% of all mutual funds failed to equal the market returns of the S&P 500. Quite a few underperformed it significantly.

4. **Being a Concentrated Investor in Businesses has Proven Lucrative for Many.** If you have ever started a business, you've already been a concentrated investor—very concentrated! You probably had the lion's share of your wealth tied up in just one company. Many of the world's most successful entrepreneurs have done exactly this—was this concentration an impediment to their financial well-being? No, because they knew their businesses well and were able to watch and follow them closely. Should the power of concentration be any less applicable to investments owned in equities?

5. **You Can't Know 100 Companies Intimately**. Finally, it seems hard to believe that the managers of funds that own 50 or 100 or 150 companies – with high yearly turnover – can be intimately familiar and close to all of the firms they own. Things at companies do change over time, and it is essential to be able to track one's holdings carefully and regularly. You can do that if you own ten to twenty companies. If a mutual fund owns 100 + stocks, the job of tracking companies is most likely delegated to subordinates - the manager is not personally on top of every holding.

If the reasoning above hasn't fully convinced you of the benefits of the "concentrated but diverse" portfolio, you might want to read *The Warren Buffett Portfolio: Mastering the Power of the Focused Investment Strategy* by Robert G. Hagstrom. Hagstrom shows, based upon simple mathematic probabilities and portfolio modeling, that it is extremely difficult to outperform the market over the long term unless your investments are focused. Show me a fund that has beaten the market over a five- year period holding 100 or more companies in its portfolio, and I'll show you one that will most likely do poorly in the next five years.

One more pertinent quote from Charlie Munger: *"We [Munger and Buffett] don't believe that widespread diversification will guarantee you anything but ordinary results. In fact, we believe that almost all really good investment records will involve relatively little diversification."*

Think of it this way: Concentration offers the possibility of achieving excellent results. Over-diversification pretty well kills that possibility. Some diversification (over different types of businesses) within the ten to twenty holdings you own is advisable. Although it may seem like an oxymoron at first, the key to smart and successful investing is the "concentrated but diverse" portfolio.

What to Expect from the "Concentrated but Diverse" Portfolio

Let's assume that you, through your financial adviser or fund manager, have chosen your equity investments wisely and have created a concentrated but diverse portfolio. What can you expect from it?

With any portfolio that is concentrated, even a well-chosen one, you can expect more day-to-day, week-to-week, and month-to-month volatility than you would see with a less-concentrated fund. If you are curious enough to look at the month-to-month results, you will undoubtedly see the composite value of the portfolio move up and down, sometimes quite a bit more than the market indices on a percentage basis. You are a long-term investor, so this should not bother you—if it does, just don't look at short term results. What matters are the long-term results. Which would you rather have over the long haul - a bumpy 20% return or a smooth 10% return?

Year-to-Year Results

Even looking at quarter-to-quarter and year-to-year results and seeing performance that varies quite a bit from the overall market does not concern me. If you look at the most successful value investors in history, you see very bumpy track records that yielded incredible long-term performance. John Maynard Keynes, in managing the Chest Fund at King's College, had an average return of over 13.2% over the 18 years from 1928 to 1945 as compared to an average return of -0.5% for the overall U.K. market through those years. Yet he underperformed the market during six of those eighteen years (33% of the time.)

When Charlie Munger ran the Charles Munger Partnership from 1962 to 1975, he outperformed the market with an average return of 24.3% compared to 6.4% average for the Dow for the same period, yet he underperformed during five of those fourteen years (36% of the time.)

Lou Simpson, who heads Geico Insurance (Geico is a wholly owned subsidiary of Berkshire Hathaway) beat the S&P 500 24.7% to 17.8%, on average, between the years of 1980 and 1996. Yet he had four years of underperformance along the way (24% of the time.)

In the short term, even great value investors can suffer from returns that under perform the market. But, in the long term, they earn higher-than-average returns for finding excellent companies that are trading below fair value. It's OK to appear to be "short-term stupid", as long as you prove to be "long-term smart."

The Trouble with Index Funds

One of the most popular index funds these days is the Vanguard Index 500. It is amazingly cheap in terms of annual fees charged to invest your money there. If you put your equity capital there, you would be sure to almost perform in line with the market (the only meaningful difference would be the small costs of the yearly fee.) If you put your money in an index fund, though, you can't effectively practice any of the three most important investment principles we've discussed. Let's go through them:

1. **The "margin of safety" principle**: Instead of buying individual companies whose fair value you have calculated and only buying them when they are available at sizable discounts to their fair value, you buy all the companies in the index all at once, at whatever price they happen to be trading at on the day you buy. In an index like the S&P 500, there may be a few out of the 500 companies which are undervalued. Seriously undervalued good companies

are rare, though, so the lion's share of stocks that you buy via the index fund will not be significantly undervalued and many may be fully valued or overvalued. Buying shares of an index fund offers little or no margin of safety.

2. **The "moat" principle**. Certainly some of the companies in the S&P 500 index enjoy sustainable competitive advantages, and a few have great ones. Still, you are buying, in effect, 500 companies without focusing only on the ones with wonderful moats. Some of the companies enjoy good moats; some do not.

3. **The "concentrated but diverse" portfolio principle.** You certainly have diversity! But you have anything but concentration.

Missing out on the power of these three critical investment principles means that you cannot expect superior performance. And you really don't expect superior performance from the S&P 500 index because you know in advance that you will be mimicking the overall market in terms of returns.

But missing the opportunity to stock your portfolio with a concentration of "A" quality ideas (with margins of safety, moats and good economics) also means that index funds, in an important sense, are actually dangerous. If you don't have the margin of safety working for you, when the market suffers a severe downturn, so do you. The S&P 500 index fell 22.1% in 2002, so your holdings in the index fund would have fallen just a little more than that (due to the fund's fees.) But you don't see how badly owners of the S&P 500 index got beaten up until you look at the whole 2000-2002 period. During that period, holders of that index lost about 50% of their value. Holders of the NASDAQ Composite Index, between 2000 and 2002, lost roughly 78%! In an index fund, there is no protection at all against the full force of the volatility of the market. The protection you get from the three major investment principles is simply not part of index fund investing.

What did the staff of index funds – and almost all mutual funds in the United States – tell investors through and after the "bad years" of 2000-2002? They tried to sell them on the idea that it was a tough break and that everybody was way down. The whole market was way down, so you should, in essence, accept it - it was "normal" to be way down. Most people, I'm afraid, bought this reasoning.

The shareholders of Berkshire Hathaway and holders of some of the great value investing funds, on the other hand, did not accept that it was "OK" to lose 50% of one's investment capital, nor did they suffer the effects. They were benefiting from all three of the major investment principles working on their behalf – especially the "margin of safety" principle. Their portfolios did not fall in value; they went up. Berkshire Hathaway stock itself went from $56,100 on January 1, 2000 to $72,750 on December 31, 2002. That's a 30% increase.

OK, tell the truth. Did you buy the line that you should be fine with having your portfolio or fund value sink way down during those years? It was hogwash. My goal in teaching you the principles of smart investing is to allow you to invest your financial assets so your investment success will not be dictated by – or much affected over the long term by - the whims of the general market. The route to that enviable position is to make sure that all three of the major investment principles are at work for you.

Owning Widely Diversified Funds When the Next Correction Hits

Buying an index fund or a mutual fund is so easy that some of you busy people will be tempted to downplay, in your mind, the dangers we just identified. You'll say to yourself something like, "I know the markets are due to have another correction eventually, but I'm going to be OK this time because ...

- "I'm invested in good companies now." Well, let's look at the Dow 30 index. There are thirty pretty decent companies in the Dow 30. What happened to the Dow-Jones Index between January 1, 2000 and December 31, 2002? It dropped 27%. Avoiding dog companies or very speculative firms helps, but it does not make you immune from a big market drop if you are invested in an index fund.

- "I'm well diversified now...I'm not real tech-heavy." That's a good thing, but, as we've seen, even the very broad diversification of the S&P 500 will not save you from a major fall. After all, the S&P 500 is pretty diversified, yet it suffered a 50% fall.

- "I'm with some different managers/different funds now." The pertinent question is ***not*** whether the managers are different, but whether they rigorously practice the principles of smart investing, especially the three major ones. Those principles, and managers who practice them effectively, are really the only protection you have against the damage a major market correction can cause to your portfolio.

So, don't fool yourself.

The big lesson in terms of "how" to manage a portfolio is "concentrated but diversified." You want good industry diversity within the group of ten to twenty wonderful companies you own.

Next, we'll address the "who" of portfolio management.

The Right Stuff

Here are the four qualities that, together, make up the "right stuff" in a great manager:

1. **Your manager is honest and intelligent.** Honesty is an absolute requirement. No question. And really effective managers don't have to be complete geniuses, but they have to be bright. If you could get a good reading on all the investment advisers and money/fund managers in America, you would find quite a few people who are intelligent enough and honest. That's not the hard part, and you shouldn't fall in love with the first manager you meet who seems smart and sincere - even if he or she wants to go golfing with you.

2. **Your manager believes deeply in and practices the principles of value investing described in this book and has a proven record of success in doing so.** Managers who practice these principles are out there, but they are not plentiful, I'm afraid. This takes some hunting, which I will help you do when we get to the next chapter.

3. **Your manager regularly follows the developments regarding each company in the portfolio.** Staying on top of all the developments that affect each holding in your portfolio is time consuming, but it is critical. Choose someone who updates the fair value of each company in your portfolio or fund, based upon all that is known, as the annual financial statements are issued and whenever the price of the stock ***seems*** to have reached full fair value.

4. **Your manager has the right temperament.** The right temperament is what really separates the consistently successful managers from the not-so-successful, in my

view. The particular temperament that you need in your manager has three components:

a. An ability to ***stay above the emotional pull of both greed and fear*** when making decisions for the portfolio. Greed and fear are powerful forces that can (adversely) affect buy, hold, and sell decisions. Remember my Abercrombie and Fitch example? It wasn't too hard purchasing the shares after they had fallen from $50 to about $18 because there was minimal fear involved. I hadn't lost anything as the stock fell. I just found it on the floor, as it were, and picked it up. But it was a lot harder to add to my holdings when it had fallen to $13. Smart investing requires dealing with facts and practicing logical, non-emotional, decision-making. You want an investment manager who can do that.

b. An ability to ***understand and stay within his or her "circle of competence."*** This is the personal trait of professional humility. Every manager has industries and businesses he or she understands and many he or she does not. Peter Lynch, famed investment manager of Fidelity's Magellan Fund (which soared when he ran it between 1977 and 1990) always preached "knowing what you own." Since no one can know everything, the trick is to find managers who are aware when they are within their circle of competence and when they are not. Now everyone has the ability to expand their circle of competence by reading and learning about an industry or business from experts they encounter. But shares of a company should not be bought in an business arena which is not within that circle of competence at the moment the purchase decision has to be made.

c. ***Patience***. There are very few great equity investment opportunities that come along in a year. A good manager patiently waits for the "fat pitch." It may only come once or twice in some years. This manager does not swing often, but when a fat pitch is coming in, he or she swings hard. This requires the patience to sit without taking action, waiting until a great company's stock sinks to a compellingly cheap price.

Patience is also necessary on the "sell" end. Selling is, in essence, harvesting. A farmer plants the crop seeds and waits for them to come up and be ready for harvest. The big difference is that in farming you know the corn will be "knee-high by the Fourth of July" and have a pretty good idea when it will be ready for picking. In equity investing, you have no idea how long it will take the market, presuming your investment hypothesis was correct, to discover a valuation mistake and move to correct it. Some companies realize their full value quickly, but the majority can take two years or more. And that requires a patient farmer.

Key Take-Home Points from Chapter 6

- **"Concentration is the key to all economic success." Take advantage of the power of concentration by building or buying into a "concentrated but diverse" portfolio.**

- **Index funds do not take full advantage of any of the three key investing principles, especially the "margin of safety" principle which recommends that companies not be purchased unless they are available at prices substantially below fair value. Index funds present, therefore, a danger of losing significant amounts of value** in a severe market correction, as witnessed from 2000 to 2002.

- A great investment manager:

  a. Is honest and intelligent

  b. Believes in and practices the principles of value investing and has a track record to prove it

  c. Follows the development of each of the companies in the portfolio regularly and closely

  d. Has the right temperament for the job (unemotional with regard to investment decisions, understanding of his or her "circle of competence", and, above all, patient.)

Chapter 7

Routes to Equity Investing

Now you're armed with a solid understanding of how "smart" equity investing should be done. It's time to think about the best way for you to get on with it. You should be clear by now that the easy routes—(1.) buying today's equivalent of the "Nifty Fifty" (the most popular, and, as a result, highest priced, fifty stocks of the moment) or (2.) sinking all your money into an index fund— are not what you want to do. If you want to get a superior return with some protection from the ravages of severe market corrections, these two are inadvisable routes.

Do it Yourself?

There is always the possibility, of course, that your interest in investing is so great that you want to manage your portfolio yourself. The "Do It Yourself" route could be successful for you if, and only if, three things are present:

1. You believe in – and practice rigorously – the principles outlined in Chapters 5, 6, and 7. This not only requires that the principles make good sense to you. It also requires that you can read financial statements well, calculate such things as owner's earnings and fair value estimates, judge when a company (based upon everything you learn through study of the business and its industry) has a solid economic moat, etc. In other words, it is one thing to believe in the principles and fervently desire that they be put to work on your behalf; it is quite another to rigorously practice them.

2. You have the temperament required for successful investing: patience, enough humility and self-awareness to stay within your circle of competence, and the emotional detachment to avoid greed or fear. My observation is that only a small percent of the population has these characteristics, so don't be too quick to give yourself a "thumbs up". Being brutally honest may save you much angst and, perhaps, a lot of money.

3. You have the time. Buying the bond ladder for your safety net, if you choose to do it yourself, is a relatively simple matter not requiring huge amounts of time. Doing equity investing correctly is a full-time job. If you really are the "busy person" this book is written for, you're contemplating nothing less than a major life shift, so be aware of that.

Unless you are going the "Do It Yourself" route, you need someone who does have the three traits enumerated above. You may already know someone who fits the bill. Be candid with yourself—does he or she really get "A" scores in each of the three areas? Later in this chapter, we will discuss some question-based approaches that may help you do a "reality check" on a potential investment manager.

Presuming you are one of the 99% of folks who do not know such a person (when you really consider all that it entails), what routes might make sense? There are four paths to at least consider. One requires very little of your time and has some things to be said for it. So let's start with it.

Route 1: Just Buying Berkshire Hathaway Stock

It would be wonderful, of course, to be able to hire the one person who has proven to be the most successful investor of all time and whose success is based upon his relentless pursuit of opportunities employing the principles of value investing. That would be Warren Buffett. Warren will probably not be interested in constructing and maintaining a portfolio for you, because he is pretty tied up maintaining his own. His "portfolio" is called Berkshire Hathaway Inc., and you can buy stock in Berkshire Hathaway on the open market. It is traded as either Berkshire Hathaway "A" shares (BRK.A) or Berkshire Hathaway "B" Shares (BRK.B).

The "A" shares have never split, and so their value has now grown, today, to about $109,000 for just one share. The "B" shares are smaller denominated shares carrying 1/100th the voting rights of an "A" share and they sell at this moment, for about $3,654. Neither stock is "cheaper" than the other in the sense of true value; they are just differently denominated for ease of trading for investors who don't want to buy shares that trade for over $100,000 each. This simple approach of just buying Berkshire Hathaway stock has two pros and two rather important cons.

The first "pro" is that, in a sense, it puts Warren Buffett to work for you, and you don't even have to pay him a fee. His work is free. And, no question, his work is good. He can judge when a company has a great moat, good economics and good management. He can calculate fair values, it is said, in his head (after he knows the facts) and he's very careful to buy a business only when it is available to him significantly below that number. He is a strong believer in the power of concentration and the "focused portfolio" and, through Berkshire Hathaway, owns some of the best businesses in the world. He has demonstrated for many years that he and his partner Charlie Munger (whose impressive wisdom you also benefit from for free) have ample patience, admirable emotional control, and the humility and self-awareness to stay within their respective circles of competence.

Secondly, buying Berkshire Hathaway stock is simple and requires almost no time to purchase and little time each year to follow the firm's fortunes going forward. The company's annual letter is all you'll need to read to keep fully abreast of its progress and challenges.

Of course, your mother was right when she told you that things that are very easy to do or free are not always as good as they seem on the surface, and buying Berkshire stock is no exception, I'm afraid. What are the cons?

First, there's the fact that Warren Buffett was born in 1930, and though he is unlikely to ever retire (he loves what he does), he will not be doing this forever. Charlie Munger was born in 1924, so he may not be around to take over the job from Warren. If Warren ever dies, it is unclear who will be making the capital allocation and investment decisions. That is not a huge concern because Berkshire has a succession plan and, although that plan has not yet been made public, I'm sure they will get someone good to manage the company. That CEO may not be as successful as Warren and Charlie have been, but I'm confident they will do pretty well. What concerns me more is what the market will do to the price of Berkshire Hathaway shares if Warren ever dies. The share price could suffer a major downturn, at least for some period of time.

The much more serious problem with buying Berkshire Hathaway stock as your route to investing is that, unless there is a huge drop in the price of the stock (probably unlikely apart from Warren's departure), you are not able to practice the "margin of safety" principle that is at the heart of value investing. You buy the whole lot of the Berkshire-owned companies and investments at whatever they are valued at on the day you buy the stock, and you can bet they will not all be "50 cent dollars."

Moreover, since Berkshire has become so massively big, with so much cash it needs to invest, it is not able to keep as concentrated a portfolio as it could when Buffett's returns were so good. It now owns all or a substantial part of some 50 companies and has about $44 billion in cash or cash equivalents burning a hole in its pocket, so that number will probably expand. In other words, Berkshire Hathaway is no longer able to take advantage of the full power of concentration.

In conclusion, buying Berkshire Hathaway stock is easy and fast, but it has some drawbacks that make it a questionable route if you want the good returns and good safety that the "margin of safety" principle brings.

Three Better Routes

There are three routes that can give you the benefits of ***all*** of the investment principles we have discussed. That's the good news. The bad news is that to find the right investment manager via any of these routes is not a quick, easy thing to do. It will take some time and effort. If you take the proper care in vetting prospective managers, however, the reward will be great: you will be able to sleep well at night, knowing that your equity investments are in the hands of a manager (or managers) with the "right stuff", using the right principles. And this is not something you will have to do on an on-going basis. It will take your attention now, and rarely, if ever, thereafter. I have numerous friends who found the right value investor through one of these routes years ago and they have become seriously wealthy as a result, while having peace of mind about their safety. The effort is worth it.

Let's look at each route:

1. <u>**The Individual Money Manager.**</u> This is a manager who constructs and maintains an investment portfolio specifically for you, and who does so in concert with all the investment principles we have discussed. Of the three routes, this is the least likely to be successful for you, for a number of straightforward reasons.

   First, good managers who understand and embrace the principles of this book are hard to find. You could interview a hundred managers who might be willing to manage an individual portfolio for you and the great majority will not follow one or more of the tenets outlined in the investment approach.

   Second, it is difficult to find a single manager, let alone a hundred, who would be willing to manage an individual portfolio for you—because it doesn't pay them enough to do so. To do the right job for you would require all the research and hard work required to run a fund of $1 billion. A manager with the inclination and real talent to be able to do that will want to do it with a very large amount of money, usually $100 million or more, so that the financial reward makes it worth the effort.

   "Individual" money managers tend to want to take you in a direction which constitutes a more efficient use of their time. Instead of running a portfolio for you, they normally advise you about investing your money in a group of mutual funds and index funds that they believe will do well for you. Then they just help you oversee that group of funds and give you advice from time to time on divesting one fund and getting into another.

Going in this direction usually means walking away from all three of the major principles we have discussed. You will not wind up with a concentrated focused portfolio. You may find yourself, through various funds, owning 150 to 250 companies. There is no taking advantage of the "margin of safety" principle, because you buy all the companies in each fund at the going rate, not by patiently waiting for a "fat pitch." And really strong and sustainable competitive advantages will most likely only be present in some of the companies you own. Not only will you forgo the advantages of the three major principles, you will pay fees at two levels: you'll pay the manager each year for helping you choose the funds and you will be paying the fees and expenses of the funds themselves.

If this is what the manager you are considering does with his or her clients, this is not the manager you need.

Now, there are still some managers around who will, in fact, be willing to run a true individual portfolio for you. If you know of one of these people and he or she has a reputation as a good value investor, you should definitely include him or her on your list of managers to consider.

2. **<u>The Manager of a "Public" Value Fund.</u>** You know what is meant by a "value" fund. By a "public" fund, I mean a mutual fund that is open to all individuals, regardless of their net worth or investment experience. You will find the particular kind of fund you want among the vast universe of mutual funds. Fair warning: there are over 11,000 mutual funds and only a small number of them are equity funds that practice all the principles of value investing we've discussed and do so in a concentrated portfolio. Mutual funds must follow rules of diversification which state that no more than 50% of the fund can be in positions of 5% or more of the fund's assets under management, so having a concentrated portfolio in a mutual fund takes some work,

if that aspect is part of the fund manager's strategy.

You may be aware of some funds that friends have recommended or you may want to research funds that might be appropriate to consider by scouring the Internet or subscribing to Morningstar's fund information. Not all the appropriate funds – funds which could possibly do a good job for you – are open to investment. The Sequoia Fund, for example, has done extremely well over many years following the principles we've discussed, but it has been closed to new investors since late 1982.

In addition, you will probably not have a chance to interview the manager of a public value fund directly to size up his or her potential to do the job for you. These managers are often managing many billion dollars and unless you're going to make it one more billion, they don't really have time to chat. You have to size them up based upon the material made available to you, including a description of the fund and its strategy, its history of performance, and a review of a year or two of quarterly fund reports, which are usually available on-line. If you have other questions that might not be answered in the materials (such as the fund's performance in a particular year when the markets suffered a major downturn), you can usually get a sales representative to get back to you with an answer.

In considering this route, I would recommend you include the following funds in your review: Bill Nygren's Oakmark Select Fund (which closed to new investors in 2002, but re-opened in 2004); Bruce Berkowitz's Fairholme Fund; Chris Davis's Clipper Fund; Ken Heebner's CGM Focus Fund; and Mason Hawkins' Longleaf Partners Fund. These are five funds which do pretty well when evaluated in accordance with the "Evaluating the Managers" section of this chapter below.

3. **<u>The Manager of a "Private" Value Fund.</u>** I am a co-manager of a private value fund, so I am partial to this route and do all my equity investing through it. "Private" means these funds are not available to just anyone. They are reserved for investment only by qualified investors. Technically, you may be considered a qualified investor if you have a net worth of at least $1.5 million, but these funds normally require a minimum investment of $500,000 or more. In practice, therefore, they are only appropriate for people with a net worth considerably higher than $1.5 million. At this writing, the SEC has proposed that the net worth of investors allowed to consider these funds be increased to $2.5 million.

   Just as good "public" value funds that I discussed above are found – very selectively – among the vast universe of mutual funds, good private value funds are found – very selectively – among a large and extremely varied universe of private funds, commonly known as "hedge funds". Hedge funds are typically open to a limited number of investors and when they reach that number (dictated by SEC regulations) no new investors are accepted.

   Referring to all private funds as "hedge funds" is an unfortunate and misleading convention. Although the term "hedge" generally refers to the hedging of risk, some of these hedge funds are very risky indeed, investing in things such as commodities, derivatives contracts, emerging market debt, and the like, often using some form of leverage (such as buying on margin) to maximize potential returns and, in some cases, practicing fast turnover "trading" – all the polar opposite of a good conservative value fund using the principles we've discussed. Also, unlike mutual funds, hedge funds are only lightly regulated. So, if you decide to invest in one of these funds, you have to be very sure you are with the right kind of manager who operates the fund just as you would run your own portfolio if you chose to do so. The great majority of hedge funds should be of no interest to you. A few of them – private funds adhering to the principals of this book – are very much worth considering.

Assets under management in this universe now total approximately two trillion dollars and a study by Institutional Investor News and HedgeFund.net reports that assets grew at the impressive rate of 24% in 2006. What's so compelling to investors about these private funds? Three things, really:

a. ***Brainpower:*** I know many of the managers of private value funds personally and, in my opinion, these funds have attracted some of the smartest, most dedicated managers in the world. In the case of the very good funds, their results have beaten the S&P 500 index by significant percentages over a long period of time, and these returns were achieved with no more exposure to risk than the overall market, and often less.

b. ***Accessibility***: Unlike managers of behemoth mutual funds, these managers are usually available for you to get to know personally and ask them enough questions to make a well-informed decision about investing with them. If you go this route, you absolutely must pursue such discussions before investing. You may need to travel to see them, but it is worth it.

c. ***Motivation***: These funds usually charge a reasonable yearly management fee to share the costs associated with managing their fund with their partners, but they also charge what is called a "performance allocation." and that allocation usually means that, in a good year, you will get 80% of the gain in value of your portfolio and they will get 20%. The result? Highly motivated

> managers. This is essentially the kind of arrangement Warren Buffett had with his partners when, in his mid-twenties, he started the Buffett Partnership (although I believe he got 25% of the upside instead of 20%). What happens when you combine a smart manager, good investment principles and great motivation? During the thirteen years of the Buffett Partnership, the average annual compounded rate of return achieved was over 30%. None of us need 30% annual returns to do well. We want to see – after the yearly fee and the cost of the performance allocations have been netted out of the return figures - that there is performance that beats the market nicely over the long term.

This combination of a smart, accessible person who uses good investment principles and is strongly motivated to perform (as opposed to just "manage") makes private value funds appealing as a route to smart equity investing.

The really difficult part about investing in a good private value fund is finding such funds to consider. Usually people learn about these funds through friends, business colleagues, or their personal tax adviser or accountant - some "private" channel. Why is that? Because, as private funds, Securities and Exchange Commission regulations prohibit these funds from advertising or promoting themselves publicly.

It is because of the these SEC regulations that it is not possible to list a few funds that you should include in your investigation here in this text, as I did with the public (mutual) funds. When someone does contact me and I have had the opportunity to assess their situation, I like to mention a number of funds that I think they should consider, but by SEC regulation I and other private fund managers are not permitted to mention anything about a private fund in a public forum. Sorry about that, but this more customized approach of taking the time to know prospective investors, their situation and their needs, is better both for you and the fund manager you choose to speak to.

Evaluating the Managers

In the case of an individual money manager or a private fund manager, you will be able to talk directly with the person who is going to be managing your investment. If you are considering investing in a mutual fund, you'll have to glean this same knowledge, as best you can, through the materials the fund provides and by talking with a sales representative.

Generally speaking, you want your manager to have an investment approach he or she can explain to you clearly, without using financial jargon that confuses you. When it comes to trusting your money to someone, you do not want to feel "baffled by BS." You want to understand what you are hearing. And, although some details might require a little explaining, you want the approach to make good basic sense to you. Did you get that feeling of things making good sense as you read through the chapters of this book? I hope so, and that's how you want to feel when you speak to the manager.

If you're considering a mutual fund and can't meet in person with the manager, take the time to read the prospectus and more than one quarterly letter to get a good picture of the manager's approach and thought process. For private funds, the quarterly fund letters to partners are normally quite revealing and I would urge you to read four or five of them, presuming you like what you learn in the face-to-face meeting with the manager.

Below are some questions that will prove helpful in vetting managers you are considering. You'll notice that sometimes the question is in the form of a question followed by the same basic question restated somewhat. This form gives the manager a little time to think about a meaningful answer and, in some cases, makes the intent of the question clearer:

1. ***When it comes to adding a company to your holdings, what are the important characteristics for that company to have? That is, what are the "must haves" you like to see in an acquisition candidate?***

Here, of course, you want to hear the manager talk about sustainable competitive advantages, good economics, good management, and, hopefully, that the fund manager won't buy until the company's stock is available at a price significantly below its fair value.

2. ***How do you determine what the fair value of a company is on a per-share basis and how big a discount to fair value do you want to see before you would consider buying the company's stock?***

   There are several ways to get a fix on fair value, from the "discounted cash flow" calculation that I use to an analysis of the sales prices of comparable companies that have been acquired by a private buyer (the way you might have real estate property appraised using "comps"), or a "sum of the parts" analysis. Just listen to the manager's explanation and see if it makes sense to you. You want to hear that they are looking for a discount – 50- or 60- or 70-cent dollars – when they buy.

3. ***What turnover of the portfolio have you experienced and what turnover should I expect going forward? What's the average length of time that a company might remain a holding in the portfolio?***

   Some turnover is fine, but you do not want to hire a manager who has a lot of portfolio turnover. Turnover is defined as the *lesser of either purchase or sales in a year divided by the average total assets for that year*. Numbers in the 20% to 30% range are considered low; 70% or more would be considered high. High turnover not only means more taxes eating away at your investment earnings, it also indicates that the manager is probably not waiting patiently to sell the portfolio's holding in line with the guidelines we have discussed.

4. ***How do you decide when it is time to sell a company? What is your thought process in deciding to sell or hold?***

   If you just stay mindful of the thoughts in Chapter 5, you'll be able to evaluate things here. Their thought process should revolve around what they estimate to be the fair value of the company and how that fair value compares to the present price of the stock.

5. ***What personal attributes do you feel are important in the manager of a portfolio? And what temperament is helpful in doing this job, do you feel?***

   Chapter 6 summarizes the sorts of things you'd like to hear in the manager's answer. In addition to intelligence and honesty, a belief in the principles of value investing and a determination to practice those principles in buying and selling is important, along with a dedication to staying in close touch with each holding's progress on a regular basis. The words you want to hear pertaining to temperament: patience, the ability to remain logical and unemotional when others are being buffeted about by fear or greed, and the self-awareness to be able to stay inside their "circle of competence" in what they consider owning.

6. ***Tell me about one or two great successes you've had with companies you have bought.***

   Listen with care and try to understand whether the success was a product of blind luck or of the strategy and principles the manager employs.

7. ***Now tell me about a situation that went bad...where your investment thesis, for some reason, did not work out. How did you handle it when it went sour?***

   What lesson, if any, did the manager learn? Did he or she seem to react out of emotion or use cool, logical decision-making?

8. ***How concentrated is your portfolio and how do you achieve diversity within that portfolio?***

   Ideally you want to see eight to fifteen – perhaps as many as twenty - holdings that are diversified among different industries or sectors.

9. ***How often do you do a complete review of each company in your portfolio? What do you to look at each time?***

   The manager should periodically re-evaluate each company's situation and profit growth prospects and re-calculate its fair value. A complete annual work-up is a must, and periodic re-evaluations, as events warrant, should be performed, as well.

10. ***Do you buy any stock on margin?***

    The answer should simply be "no", in my opinion. Using leverage to buy stocks is a risk you would be unwise to take.

11. ***What is the inception date of the fund? What is your official performance, net of all fees (and performance allocation, in the case of a private fund) since inception and what is the return of the S&P 500 over that exact same period, including all***

dividends that would have been received reinvested?

As attorneys are quick to point out, "past performance is no guarantee of future success." But I believe that past performance, especially when there is a five-year or more history of it with the same manager or managers who are going to be working for you, is a decent indicator of the manager's ability to add value past what you could achieve by investing in an index fund.

I like to look at "since inception" numbers because they are for the longest period over which you can judge the value that the manager has brought to the fund. He may have had a good quarter or the last year may have been stellar, but what really counts is how well the fund has done in the long term, so don't be dazzled by any shorter term numbers. Once you have the official numbers, calculate this simple ratio:

$$\frac{\textbf{Fund's return since inception}}{\textbf{S\&P Return over the same period}}$$

Let's assume the fund's return over the period was 10% and the return of the S&P was 8%. Then the ratio is 10/8 or 1.25. The manager has done ***25% better*** than the S&P after all it cost the fund members to have the manager run the fund on their behalf. That's very good. This ratio is an important reflection of the value the manager has added. If the fund doesn't have ***some*** value added past what the index fund could have done, why hire that manager?

12. ***During a tough year, when the stock market overall declined significantly (2002, for example), how did the fund fare? What was the fund's return that year after all fees and expenses (and performance allocation) compared to the S&P's performance?***

In my opinion, this is the most important number you need to see about any fund you study, public or private. If the most important thing about making money is not losing it, this tells the story, without extraneous rhetoric. It tells you how well the fund held up in a major market downturn. For 2002, containing the loss to less than 10% would have been decent, containing it to less than 5% would have been quite good, and having lost nothing (or having actually made money) would have been the kind of outstanding performance you are seeking.

Here are a few additional questions for managers of private funds, presuming such funds are appropriate for you to consider:

1. ***How much of the manager's own money is in the fund?*** Do they "eat their own cooking", in other words?

2. ***Are they audited yearly***? That's an important thing in an industry that is only lightly regulated.

3. ***Are they SEC Registered?*** It does not assure you of a lot, but it's better than no registration. If they are SEC registered, every five years or so SEC representatives are likely to give them a good looking over, which could not hurt.

4. ***Do they get a performance allocation even when their performance is below some minimum threshold?*** I don't like the idea of paying a performance allocation in a bad year. If I could have made more return keeping my money in a money market or savings account, I don't think the manager deserves any kind of payday other than the basic management fee of 1%. So I like to see some mechanism in place, usually called a "hurdle rate," below which there

is no performance allocation for that year. I don't mind seeing the manager have a huge payday in a great year, but I think some restraint is in order when the return is small.

In the case of an individual money manager (one who is intending to build an individual portfolio for you as opposed to a fund manager), personal references, of course, are critical. There is no fund record to go on, so the feelings that the manager's clients have toward his or her work are all you have to go on, other than what he or she has to say.

Likewise, in private value funds, it is a good idea to get the names and numbers of a few partners in the fund who might be amenable to receiving a call from a new prospective partner. Someone who has been the manager's partner for a while has insights from which you might benefit.

Key Take-Away Points from Chapter 7

- **Other than the "full-time job" that managing your own investments involves, there are four possible routes to investing in equities along the lines we have discussed. One is the quick and easy route of just purchasing and holding Berkshire Hathaway stock, but that has some important downsides, primarily the fact that you miss the opportunity to concentrate your investment on nothing but seriously undervalued companies.**

- **The three "better routes" we outlined include:**

    - **Hiring the right manager to select and oversee an individual portfolio for you using all the principles we have discussed**

- Investing in a "public" (mutual) value fund with the right manager

- Investing in a "private" value fund with the right manager (presuming you are a qualified investor)

• Use the twelve questions in this chapter to carefully vet any manager with whom you are considering investing.

Chapter 8
Three Little Fund Secrets

If, studying possible routes for equity investing as discussed in the last chapter, you discover a good fund – or multiple funds – you will doubtless do well. But there are three important secrets which can improve your returns when you invest in equity funds, and, more importantly, provide some protection from a severe market downturn. Let's discuss each one.

1. The Right Number of Funds

As the number of companies you own in a portfolio grows, the more your portfolio behaves like an index fund. So how many funds should you own? Holding a portfolio of ten to twenty companies gives you the best chance to achieve great returns, as we discussed in depth in Chapter 7. Focusing on ten to twenty of the most undervalued companies also helps you avoid the fate that is common to all broad index funds: when there is a severe market downturn, they fall right along with it.

If you invest in five good funds and each of those funds were to own twenty companies each, you have a problem. Between all five funds there will undoubtedly be some overlap in companies owned, so you may not own a hundred companies, but you could easily wind up owning eight-five or ninety companies across all the funds. Whoops! You just inadvertently created an index fund for yourself. Too much diversification, not enough concentration.

Instead, if you have identified five good funds that fit all the criteria we have discussed, size up carefully how good each one is, perhaps using a numerical scale like they use with the quality of wine, where 100 is absolutely tops. You could assign a range of points for such items as:

- the history of the fund's performance in a very tough year
- by what percent the average annual compounded rate of return of the fund beat the S&P index since inception of the fund
- how well you think the fund has done in employing the key value principles such as "margin of safety"
- your impression of the manager's temperament
- how concentrated the portfolio is
- how much "skin" the manager has in the game with respect to his own money

Let's say when you consider everything, the fund at the top of your list gets a total score of 98, and it has ten to fifteen companies in its portfolio at any one time. The next fund down the list gets a score of 95 and holds about ten to fifteen companies, the third fund scores 93 and holds fifteen to twenty companies, etc. Now that you have sorted your options, I suggest you put your money into just the top two funds. You want to wind up investing in no more than about thirty companies in all. In fact, there is a lot to be said for using the power of concentration yourself and putting a higher percentage of your investment capital in the very top fund. If you are very sure that the top fund deserves that "98" score you gave it, you could make a strong argument for investing all your money into it—but not until you have had some experience with the fund for a couple of years and are able to corroborate your initial high rating.

Does the idea of only being in one or two funds worry you? If you don't remember all the good reasons for maintaining a concentrated portfolio, do yourself a big favor at this point and review the first five pages of Chapter 7.

As long as the funds they choose are good value funds, people who keep their portfolio of equity investments concentrated get better results and are better protected against market downturns.

2. The Best Investment Timing

Most of you are probably aware that it is impossible to "time the market." You never know when the market is going to go up or down in the short term and traders who try to time the market, sooner or later, lose a bundle. But there is one aspect of fund investing that is a bit different.

Do you know when most people get into a particular fund? They jump in when they read about a hot streak that the fund has had. They see that it has been up 20% per year for the last three years and they can't wait to invest, imagining the 20% per year streak will go on and on. But what really happens?

If a fund has some history, you can calculate how much better than the S&P index it has performed over the long term. You are not going to bother with funds which, netting out all expenses and fees, don't do somewhat better than the S&P 500, so for the funds in which you may want to invest, this performance difference will be expressed as a positive percentage. Let's imagine the average annual yearly performance for a fund in question is 25% better than the S&P index. So in the average year, if the S&P were up 10%, this fund would be up about 12.5%.

You may recall from a college probability or statistics course that one of the great laws of nature is that things tend to revert to the norm over the long term. If housing prices in a section of your town have risen an average of 8% per year over the past 30 years, that sets a norm for housing price increases one might expect going forward, unless something fundamental changes. If, without any significant changes, they have risen 15% over each of the last two years, the probability that housing prices will experience slower than 8% growth (or maybe even a contraction) goes up. In other words, when you see a period of over-performance, you can rationally expect that there will soon be a period of under-performance so that – over the long term – the norm will be reflected in the averages.

It doesn't make sense, therefore, to jump into funds that have just gone through a particularly hot growth spurt, yet people do it all the time. Greed is egging them on, and it's likely that they will soon be its victims, as the fund's performance returns to its norm. I know an investor who has consciously decided to take advantage of the fact that performance tends to revert to the norm long term. As he makes additional investments into his fund, he holds off until the fund has a quarter during which it under-performs the S&P 500. That's when he invests the additional money, figuring that performance will revert to the norm (in his favor) and soon the fund will outperform the index. Funds rise and fall as their holdings and investment strategies either bear fruit or don't (yet). The timing of these fluctuations is not knowable in advance, but it is pretty clear in hindsight (through observing the temporary underperformance), so this approach works quite well.

Let's return to our example of the hypothetical fund that, on average over the long term, outperforms the market by 25% per year. You do the math…what number do you need in year #3 in each scenario to make the three-year average come out to +25%? In each case Year #1 outperforms, as usual, by 25%. In the "growth spurt" case on the left, the fund has the good fortune to outperform by 75% in Year #2. In the case on the right it ***underperforms*** by 25% in Year #2.

	A Growth Spurt Year #2	A Slow Year #2
Year #1 :	25% Better Than the S&P	25% Better Than the S&P
Year #2 :	75% **Better** Than the S&P	25% **Worse** than the S&P
Year #3 :	?	?

If the performance reverts to the norm of 25% per year within this three-year period, then Year #3 in the "Growth Spurt" example has to be -25% (a 25% under-performance). In the "Slow Year" example it has to be +75% (75% over-performance of the S&P.)

The lesson is simple: It is wise to make additional investments to a fund right after a period in which the fund underperformed its normal return, especially if it is lagging the indices.

3. Funds That Have "Insurance Policies"

A good value fund provides two forms of defense against a precipitous market downturn, and some provide a third. Let me explain.

The two forms of defense good value funds have working for them are...

1. They buy companies that are significantly undervalued, so they enjoy the protective effect of the "margin of safety" in good times, and in bad. This alone helped many of the best value funds avoid much or any loss in years that the market performed poorly, such as 2002.

2. They buy companies with good economics (low debt-to-equity ratios and interest payments on debt which they can easily handle, even when the pressure is on, for example.) This enables the companies in their portfolios to weather severe storms so that any capital losses in portfolio value will not be permanent losses.

Some funds also provide an additional "insurance policy" in the form of what are called "long-dated puts." A "put" option is a financial contract between two parties, the buyer and the seller (the "writer") of the option. The put allows the owner (the fund, in this case) the right, but not the obligation, to ***sell*** some asset —such as a number of shares of stock —to the "writer" at a certain time (the "exercise date") for a certain price (the "strike price".) The "writer" assumes the obligation, through this contract, to purchase the asset at the "strike price." Long-dated put options are puts that have their exercise dates fairly far into the future, usually about two years out.

A put option can act as an insurance policy against severe market downturns. Let's say that the fund has identified four companies that its manager believed were highly over-valued. The manager would expect that the price of these companies would come down to more realistic levels even without a big market downturn and that with a severe downturn they would go way down. This would eliminate from consideration such companies as an over-valued gold-mining company, for example, because in the case of a big market downturn, the price of gold might soar and the gold mining company's stock might rise in lock-step with the value of the underlying metal.

Now let's imagine that the fund invests 1% of its assets into the long-dated (two-year) put options of each of those four companies, so it has a little portfolio of four long-dated put contracts among its list of normal holdings. To make the math easy, let's further imagine that when the put purchases were made each of the four companies happened to be priced (overpriced, the fund manager feels) at $50 per share. Let's also posit that the long-dated puts have a strike price of $45, and that the puts cost the fund $5 per share.

If the exercise date comes and goes and the price of those companies never declines, what has holding the puts cost the fund (i.e., what's the worst that could happen to the fund's returns because of this purchase of long dated puts)? If all the stocks slowly moved up to $70 in price over the life of the puts, no money could be made on the puts and they would expire worthless. How bad is that? They gave protection to the fund (as we'll see in a moment) for two years and 4% of the fund's assets were dedicated to them, so it cost an average of 2% of return per year - not too bad. If the fund could have returned 15% yearly growth over those two years (without the put protection), it will, instead, have a 13% annual return. Holding puts in this type of scenario is like paying the premium on a fire insurance policy. If the house doesn't burn down, you're still out the cost of the premium, but you were able to sleep well at night in the meantime.

If the house does burn down, you'll be glad your fund gave up a small percentage of its return to hold those puts. In our example, let's say the market suffers a 20% correction and the value of the four companies on which the long-dated puts were written falls 40% (because they had been so egregiously over-valued previously.)

As of the exercise date of the put contracts, their prices are each $30 per share. The fund's put contracts specify that the writer has agreed to purchase the shares at $45, even though they have fallen to $30. The fund makes $15 per share for a $5 per share investment (the cost of the puts.) This is 200% return in two years. In fact, if the fund manager was right about these specific companies being over-valued, the fund could benefit from a sizable drop in the stock's price (and a rise in the value of the puts) even if the market as a whole doesn't turn down at all.

Since the fund initially invested 4% of the assets into these puts, it has enjoyed an 8% gain in asset value as a result. And it comes in the form of cash, just when the market is down 20% (i.e., when the prices of a lot of good companies have been seriously beaten up – a wonderful time to buy in most cases). When the house actually burns down, it's nice to have had insurance.

Should you run out and buy a basket of long-dated puts? No. The fund manager whom you trust to evaluate and find exceptionally ***under***-valued companies is the individual I would trust to identify exceptionally ***over***-valued companies, and this whole strategy – the value of this insurance policy, if you will - is totally dependent upon that ability.

Key Take-Away Points from Chapter 8

- **Don't invest in too many funds – even good ones – or you will lose the power of concentration in your investments. Go with the one or two best choices after you have carefully considered them all.**

- **The best time to invest in a fund (or add to your previous investment in it) is often at a time when it has just had a period of underperforming the indices (as opposed to its usual over performance) – not when it has been on a hot streak.**

- **Value funds guard against the effects of serious market corrections by their very nature – buying companies very selectively and only when those companies are already far undervalued. Some funds add another layer of protection by holding a group of long-dated puts to act as additional "insurance" against large market downturns.**

Chapter 9

Real Estate Investing

We've discussed how to do equity investing "the right way" for the last five chapters. While you've learned the basic principles to guide you with intelligent and safe investment in stocks, you have also learned the principles that will serve you well in your real estate investments, even if the only real estate you ever chose to invest in is your home. We will discuss the principles in a moment, but first, as we did with equity investing, let's think about how you can make money with real estate...because here things are a little different.

The principal route to making your wealth grow by investing in equity is appreciation. Your wealth grows as the prices of the stocks you own rise. Dividends are an additional source of wealth, but the real growth engine is appreciation.

How You Can Make Money with Real Estate

Of course, price appreciation is also a major wealth engine in real estate investing, but there are other ways to make good money in real estate, even if the price of the property you buy doesn't appreciate at all. The reason for this is simple: if you own a good piece of property – like a wonderful lot for a home site or a beautiful summer home– that property has, in most locations, zero chance of disappearing or going bankrupt (unlike a company). It will be around for years to come. Though its value may rise or fall, it is not going vanish altogether. Over the long term, its value is highly likely to appreciate. For this reason, it is normally safe to use some leverage to buy good real estate. That is, you can borrow a fairly large part of the cost of the property, if you choose to, just making a down payment of some reasonable amount.

In their informative book *Investing in Real Estate*, authors Andrew McLean and Gary W. Eldred capture the essence of the advantage of leverage in this scenario, which illustrates why you don't need appreciation to profit from purchasing real estate:

> *Assume that you pay $250,000 for a property today. You put $50,000 down and finance the balance of $200,000 over 20 years. During this total period, your rent collections give you no surplus cash return. They merely cover your property expenses and pay off your mortgage. The price of the property doesn't go up. You sell at the end of year 20 for $250,000 – exactly the same amount you paid. Even without an increase in this property price, you have multiplied your original investment of $50,000 fivefold.*

That's pretty impressive, but what's more impressive is that it would be a rare case indeed that didn't see the value of a real estate property – particularly if you bought it "right" in the first place – go up at all over a period as long as twenty years! If the value of the property doubled every ten years, for example, that would be just over a 7% annual price appreciation—nothing unusual these days. Doubling every ten years would mean this hypothetical property's price at the end of twenty years would be $1 million. What would that make the return on your $50,000 investment? It would have grown twenty-fold. Now you see how investment in good real estate can be a tremendous wealth engine, just as ownership of wonderful businesses can.

Although the use of leverage is certainly the other major way (besides price appreciation) that one makes money in real estate, it is not the only one. Real estate can give you a steady stream of income that may be greater than the cost of the mortgage and property maintenance. You can create value in your property by making some judicious improvements to it. And, if you have borrowed money to buy the property, you gain by having the inevitable reality of inflation cheapen the dollars with which you pay back that mortgage.

Doing Real Estate "The Right Way"

If you have read about and understood the last five chapters of this book, you are now clear about the "right way" to invest in equities and you, therefore, also know and understand the principles that will allow you to invest wisely in real estate. Let's review six key concepts of smart investing and examine how they apply to real estate investing:

1. **The "Moat" Idea / Scarcity.** When we discussed buying good companies, we started with the idea that the really desirable ones – the ones that would provide the biggest long-term profit growth, the greatest returns on investment, and the greatest safety for your investment – were those that had sustainable competitive advantages, or "moats." There is a direct parallel in real estate that I call the "Scarcity Principle." Here's an example:

   Over the years I have bought quite a few vacant-but-developed (utility-ready) lots on which a family could build a home. One year I bought a group of five lots in a very nice development area – very high end – where I thought I could not lose money in the long run. One of the lots was larger than the others and larger than almost any lot in the development. It also had a beautiful view off a hillside of a huge panorama that included all the city lights at night. I had bought the lots just to turn around and sell them at a profit. What lot did I sell first? You guessed it, the big lot (with a very big price tag, by the way). It sold at a 45% profit in about twelve months. The other four lots, however, were run-of-the-mill lots in this development, and there were about sixty-plus lots similar to them. They were not "scarce." It took me five years to unload the last of those four lots and because I had to pay taxes and association dues while I held them, the average annual return for those lots was only about 8% per year.

Scarcity is a beautiful thing. In another part of my town some years earlier, I was out for a ride one day and, up on a bluff overlooking 14,000 foot Pike's Peak from an impressive vantage point, I saw the last two lots of a development sitting side-by-side in the middle of the west-facing side of the bluff. They had been priced pretty much like every other lot in the development – about $40,000 back then. As people bought up the other lots, these remaining two lots had become a scarcer commodity. I thought that, joined together into one lot, they might make a spectacular place to build a home for myself and my family some day. So I bought them both, thinking I'd hold them for a few years until I would have time to think about building. After the purchase, I took all "For Sale" and other signs off the lots, and proceeded to forget about them.

I was only able to forget them for about three weeks. Soon, other people who were driving by saw and appreciated the lots and their rarity and started having realtors call me to see if I would sell. Keep in mind that I didn't even have a sign on the property. These people had to go to the city records and look me up. That's how much interest they had.

This Scarcity Principle (the "Moat" idea) is as powerful in real estate investing as it is in equity investing. When what you own is rare and your potential customers understand that "there's nothing else quite like it" (at least in the particular city or area) you, as the owner, are in a strong profit-making position.

2. **The "Margin of Safety" Principle.** Calculating the fair value of a property is not a simple task, just as it takes some effort to get an accurate fair value estimate for a company. Yet we've seen that developing an estimate of the fair value of a company is absolutely essential to understanding whether and when to buy or sell its stock. Without a good fair value estimate you have no compass to guide you and are, essentially, lost and guessing in the dark. Not good.

   The same is true in real estate. If you can work up a reasonable estimate of the fair value of the property, based on "comps" (comparative prices paid for similar properties), you have a compass. The lesson here is the same as with equities: you want to buy properties only when you can buy them significantly below their fair value. In order for a piece of real estate to properly appreciate to its full fair value, you might have to make some improvements to the property, but if you understand that (and perhaps others do not) you have an "edge," an advantage, as a buyer.

   There is a gentleman in my town who now owns one of the best home lots anywhere in Colorado. The lot itself and the view from it are spectacular. Yet some years ago it was selling below its fair value, in this fellow's mind because, when he and all the other potential buyers were looking at it, it had on it one of the uglier homes in the state— so ugly that it blinded people to the lot's full potential. But it didn't blind him. He bought it, "scraped" the old house away, and revealed the property's full potential. People were amazed.

Just as with equities, if you are buying at what you believe is full fair value, you have no "margin of safety," and if your estimate of that fair value turns out to be too optimistic, you could get burned. If you purchase a property when it is clearly priced ***over*** its full fair value, you are not investing; you are speculating. You are gambling that some "greater fool" will overpay even more extravagantly in the future. As they say in Vegas, "Good Luck!"

3. **The "Concentration" Principle.** Remember Peter Drucker's maxim, "Concentration is the key to all economic success." Real estate investing is no exception to this rule, especially if you are a busy person. You don't have time to keep track of a large group of real estate properties, so you need on focus on just the best opportunities.

4. **The Need to Invest with a Long Term Perspective.** A stock of a publicly traded company that you buy on Monday can be sold on Tuesday via the stock market—it is a "liquid" investment. Real estate is simply not as liquid as equities are. If you buy real estate, you need to be prepared to hold it for the long haul. Ideally, you want to hold your equity investments long-term, too, but you can unload them easily if you need to raise cash. A piece of property, on the other hand, could go unsold for months or even years. So, before you buy property, you have to make sure that you can comfortably service the costs of owning it – taxes, debt service, association dues, maintenance, etc. - when netted out against whatever income, if any, the property can reasonably be expected to produce, for the

long haul. Then, and only then, will you be prepared to invest in that real estate properly. If you have bought good real estate that has some scarcity working for it and you have bought it somewhat below its fair value, then letting time work for you is tremendously to your advantage.

5. **The Need for Patience.** We have discussed the fact that a portfolio manager making equity investments needs to have the patience to wait until a desirable company can be bought significantly below fair value. The manger must also have the patience to give each holding in the portfolio time to grow to its full fair value.

   Patience pays off in real estate investing, too. One of the best investments I ever made was in a summer home I purchased at Lake Tahoe in 1993. I vacationed for a few weeks each year in the Tahoe area for fifteen years before making this purchase. It's a great place for a summer getaway not only because of its incredible natural beauty and recreation opportunities, but also for its lack of mosquitoes and wonderful weather from June to November (almost all of the precipitation in the Tahoe Basin happens outside of those months.) While it is sweltering everywhere else in America, Tahoe normally stays dry, very comfortable, and sparklingly sunny. It's a freak of nature.

   For the first eight or nine years that my family and I vacationed there, I would travel around the lake in search of the best possible place to buy. I didn't want a big home (too much maintenance when you live in Colorado), but I wanted something very beautiful and special and I wanted to be close enough to the lake to spit in it. It's the Scarcity Principle at work. "Right on the Lake" properties are more rare and desirable, much more so than the many layers of homes off the lake. It takes about two hours to drive around Lake Tahoe, so considering all the possible home developments was no quick task, but I searched patiently and finally came to the conclusion that the very best spot was a development called Chinquapin, about three miles East of Tahoe City, on the California side. It is spectacular.

Did I buy there? Not right away. In studying values and prices, I came to the conclusion that properties there were fully priced, so I just started renting every summer, and waited. And waited. And, finally, in 1993, certain Silicon Valley companies came under severe pressure. As a result, a unit became available at Chinquapin for what I thought was a price below its fair value. I thought there was a chance the seller was "motivated" enough to have some flexibility, so I sent in an offer that was about a 30% discount to fair value (I could have waited for a 50% discount, but it might not have happened in my lifetime) and the seller accepted. Patience paid off, just as it does in equity purchases.

6. **The Need to Stay Within Your "Circle of Competence."** In that last example, if I had not known enough about real estate values of "Right on the Lake" properties at Lake Tahoe during that period, how could I have been able to estimate what the home in Chinquapin was worth? Go outside your circle of competence in real estate, and you do so at great peril. Your circle of competence may be different from mine. You may know a lot about ranch land and how it can be subdivided profitably, for example. There are many different circles of competence when it comes to real estate. Because you can purchase an individual property using a reasonable (say 20%) down payment and borrowing the rest, you could consider taking advantage of your expertise - but only when the property is also "scarce" and priced below fair value.

Routes to Your Real Estate Investing

The problem with many forms of real estate investing is that they require lots of time and work to do correctly, and you are a busy person. So let's consider the avenues that do not take much time or work.

The first route is the occasional purchase of property that I have written about above. I bought lots or home properties that made very good returns when they were well within my circle of competence, had the great benefit of being "scarce," and were available for a price I had estimated was significantly below fair value. I bought only a small number at any one time, so that I had a concentrated portfolio, if you will, of real estate and I only bought them because I knew I was going to be able to cover all expenses associated with them from year to year until they sold.

If you are a busy person, you probably should rule out all but two additional types of real estate investing, because most require too much time and attention. And one of those two, in my opinion, is not advisable. The two are:

1. Purchasing Real Estate Investment Trust shares (REITs)
2. Investing in a good private real estate partnership or fund.

Let's look at each.

REITs

Real Estate Investments Trusts can be either public or private, but, in all cases, you are buying shares in a firm that owns and usually manages, buys, and sells, real estate properties. One feature that differentiates a REIT from other companies in which you could buy shares is that designation as a REIT essentially eliminates corporate income taxes. The downside is that REITs are required to distribute 90% of their income each year. That income may be taxable once it gets to you, the investor.

I think investing in REITs is, in most cases, inadvisable. We have come through a period, since mid-2000, when the S&P Index went way down, came way back, and is not quite back to the heights it reached in 2000. What have the REIT indexes done during this period? The Vanguard REIT Index Fund Investor Shares (VGSIX), for example, was priced at about $12 in mid-2000 and it has risen, almost without stopping for breath, to $26.51. It's up 120%, roughly, while the S&P Index has not grown, over the same period, at all. This kind of super-achieving growth in price is not the stuff of which under-valuation is made. I look for investments with prices that have been beaten up, not pumped up to unbelievable heights versus the market. So at present REITs are particularly unattractive. But let's consider the argument for ***never*** buying them.

REITs are shares in a company. And the only time to buy a company is when it is priced below its fair value. Only when you are quite sure the company is being priced significantly below fair value do you have a good margin of safety. The problem is, how do you know what the fair value of a REIT company is? How do you know the real fair value of the shifting group of real estate assets being held at any one time by the REIT?

Honestly, I have no idea. There is no really dependable way to accurately estimate the value of those assets. This is why I have never chosen to invest in REITs. I don't mind that I missed the ride up over the last six years. I have had a nice ride up with other investments I consider safer. Not being in REITs, I'll also miss the ride down and would advise you to do the same.

Investing in a Good Private Real Estate Partnership or Fund

The final possible route to real estate investment is to get involved with a private real estate entity run by a manager. These are typically set up in two ways:

1. As a partnership that allows you to invest in one particular property.
2. As a fund, giving you ownership in a diversified set of properties.

If you were to invest in one set up as a partnership, you would need to build some diversity by investing in several partnerships, either through the same manager or a couple of different ones you have come to respect. No manager, regardless of how good he or she is, earns great returns on ***every*** project. Some are great winners and some are disappointments, so having adequate diversity in these kinds of investments is a must.

Let's compare these real estate ventures with the ***equity*** funds we have discussed in previous chapters. When you invest in an equity fund, you are not so much buying the companies that the fund owns (because they change from year to year) as the abilities you believe the fund manager possesses and will use on your behalf. In the case of real estate partnerships or funds, you are investing your money into both the manager and the particular property or set of properties that are to be developed in some way.

In a real estate partnership or fund, therefore, there is the question of "who" you are investing with and "what" they are investing in. Both aspects are important to evaluate.

Although both matter, in a real estate partnership or fund the "who" matters a lot more than the "what" —simply because buying (and managing) real estate assets is a lot more complex than purchasing stock. You need to feel comfortable with the person who will handle the purchase negotiations, the development or renovation, the management, and the eventual sale of the property. If the "who" is the right person practicing the right value investment principles we have covered, they will generally buy into good opportunities. But with real estate deals something almost always goes a bit (or a lot) wrong. Something happens that was not expected. Then your salvation and eventual profit is totally dependent on the "who." Good people will manage through the problems; lesser managers may not.

If you want to take advantage of this kind of real estate investment, you need a good way to find and then evaluate both the "who" and the "what."

Finding and Evaluating Good Real Estate Partnership and Fund Managers

These deals, particularly the really good ones put together by truly talented managers, are not easy to find because those in the know fill up the limited subscription quickly. The best managers have track records of very impressive results, so that many people may have their names in for the next available deal. The best way to find possible managers of good real estate partnerships is to ask a trusted accountant in one of the bigger firms in your area or to ask friends and business associates if they are aware of any. Accountants usually know which managers have good reputations because they see the deals being done by their clients. If you are able to get these managers' names and contact them, you can ask to be reached next time there is a new partnership or fund available for investment.

When an opportunity presents itself, you need an evaluation system. I worked with Buck Blessing, one of the most successful managers of private real estate partnerships and funds that I know, to develop a way to tell the good from the bad. After all, it takes one to know one. We'll start with the most important part.

Evaluating the "Who"

1. ***What is the manager's track record?*** There is no public data available for real estate partnerships or funds, so you have to ask the manager for a report that contains results, in terms of annualized returns for each project they have done. A few things are crucial in this review. Make sure the manager shows you the results of ***all*** the deals that have been done – all those where the gain has been realized and all those that have not closed yet - not just a few that the manager has selected. It's fine and quite natural for some of the deals to have had disappointing results, but you need to see them all. When you spot investments that have not performed well, ask the manager why they did poorly and what he learned from that.

   You also want to make sure the return results are stated net of all fees, expenses, and performance allocation (the percent that goes to the manager, sometimes called the "promote".) It's also helpful to compare, on a project-by-project basis, the actual return versus the originally projected return.

   It is preferable if the manager has audited returns, of course, but not all will have those.

2. ***Where does the manager generally engage in projects?*** Real estate is fundamentally a regional business. If a manager lives in Colorado, but engages in deals in Phoenix and other remote locations, that would be a concern. Generally it's best to go with managers who stay within their circle of competence (as with equity managers), and there are natural geographical limitations to competence in real estate.

3. ***What has been the manager's experience with the kind of project being proposed in this particular partnership?*** You don't want this to be his or her first time managing this type of property or partnership.

4. ***What is the manager's process of due diligence on acquisitions?*** The due diligence should be very extensive, right down to counting each and every parking space around a building to make sure no misrepresentations have been made.

5. ***What is this manager's reputation among people who have invested with him or her?*** The manager may be a "nice person", but what you care about is honesty and capability to do two things: (1.) manage the investment effectively and (2.) communicate in a forthright and understandable way to the partners. The best way to get an idea of these attributes is by speaking with partners the manager has had or has presently. Get a list of partners and contact information and do a little homework. Few investors do this, but real estate investments are usually pretty long term. It is worth a little effort up front to make sure you are getting into this with a solid manager. Ask the partners about their experience with the manager, why they keep investing with him or her if they do, and how happy they are with the reporting the manager makes available. You might also read a quarterly report or two to get an idea if you are comfortable with the depth of communication.

6. ***What fee structure does the manager use?*** The structure will vary somewhat from deal to deal, but you want to make sure you're dealing with someone who is not charging excessive fees. Managers are running businesses

and it's reasonable for them to charge fees for various services in a real estate deal. But you'll want to get up-to-date estimates of the going market rate for things like property management fees, asset management fees, and construction management fees, as they may be involved in the situation you are considering.

Evaluating the "What"

If your study of the manager leaves you feeling negative or unconvinced, there is no point in studying the deal itself. But if you feel sure of the "who," you can move on to the "what."

1. ***Is there a clearly defined investment strategy for this project that makes good sense to you?*** It really all starts with this question. Presuming the manager is a good one, he or she should be able to articulate the strategy so that you come away well-informed and persuaded of its likelihood of achieving the return objective. There is no magic in real estate investing. The deal has to make sense. If it doesn't make sense to you, it probably doesn't make sense.

2. ***What percent of the return is expected as a result of cash flow (rents, etc.) and what percent is expected to come from price appreciation?*** Return from cash flow is more predictable and reduces the risk of a deal. In any case, debt service on the property should not exceed cash flow.

3. ***What is the expected time line of the project?*** How long will your money be tied up and what kind of liquidity and cash flow can you expect from it until the property

ultimately sells? Make sure you are comfortable with this. Once in, this is usually something you're into for many years. You can't call and ask for your investment to be returned any time you like, as you can with many equity funds.

4. ***Is the project a type of recreational real estate?*** Properties in nice recreation areas have a decided advantage. There is a huge transfer of wealth going on in this country now – often moving from older folks who were frugal to younger loved ones who don't mind investing some of the money in a nice lifestyle. This will most likely ensure that properties in or near upscale resort and recreational areas will continue to escalate handsomely for the next twenty to thirty years or more. Think waterfront lots, ski areas, ranch land, etc.

5. ***Is the manager's motivation aligned with yours as the investor?*** The first thing you want to see is that the manager has plenty of "skin in the game." On smaller deals, this may mean he or she is investing 5-10% of the full deal. On larger ones it may be a lower percentage, but still money big enough that they wouldn't want to write it off if the deal failed. Fees in line with the going market rates are something else you want to see. You don't want the manager getting rich if you aren't. Make sure you understand any conflicts of interest the manager may have in this particular investment, and decide whether they are manageable.

6. ***Does the deal involve making recourse loans?*** If so, it's a major negative. You want to risk your equity, but you do not want to personally guarantee the loan. Let someone else do that.

7. ***Is the performance allocation, or the "promote," reasonable and appropriate?*** The split of the upside to the manager is usually between 20% and 50%, depending upon the amount of work the manager must do to realize the gain. A stable, cash-flowing, existing asset is usually lower risk and doesn't take much work, for example, so a fair split might be 20% to the manager once the entire invested amount plus 6% annual return has gone to the investors. A ground-up raw development deal is riskier and takes a lot of work, so a fair split might be 50% to the manager once the entire invested amount plus a 12% annual return has gone to the investors.

Key Take-Away Points from Chapter 9

- **Real estate investing offers the potential of excellent long-term returns due not only to price appreciation, but also to the ability to borrow a significant proportion of the property's purchase price, thus leveraging the effect of each investment dollar.**

- **The investment principles you need to observe to be successful with real estate (the importance of "scarcity", the "margin of safety" principle, the need to stay within your "circle of competence, etc.) have direct parallels in the world of equity investing.**

- **REITs, especially in these days of high valuation, do not present an attractive route to real estate investing if safety is important to you.**

- **In addition to investing in individual properties you feel confident will grow in value, consider a private real estate partnership or fund. If so, the six questions to vet** the manager and the seven questions about specific real estate projects given in this chapter will prove helpful.

Chapter 10

Questions from Busy People

This chapter is made up of answers to the twelve questions I'm asked most often by busy people who care about investing smartly. The topic is underlined in each case so that you can quickly find answers to the questions that interest you most.

Question #1:

When it comes to investing in equities, should I include some <u>foreign stocks</u> in my portfolio by incorporating one fund that specializes in that?

If a good fund you invest in owns some foreign companies, that's fine. But there is no need to actively seek out and include a fund that only invests in foreign companies. Many of the better US-based companies you will come to own in your portfolio are already global businesses. At Coke, for example, foreign sales account for 66% of net sales and 76% of annual profits. Coke is ubiquitous the world over. International Game Technologies sells its gaming machines not just in Las Vegas and Atlantic City, but wherever gaming is legalized all over the world. And unlike some foreign companies, US companies are required by law to report financial information to investors through a relatively easy to understand, consistent accounting system.

You may see particular foreign markets get "hot" from year to year (particularly in the very volatile world of "emerging markets"), but they can also turn very cold. The best fund managers look for the most outstanding opportunities for dependable profit generation, and US-based companies provide plenty of opportunity to build your wealth, as well as some global diversification.

Question #2

Is it important to stay invested? Does this mean I should never take money from my account?

Ideally you want to keep the bulk of your money invested, but you don't need to go overboard.

A study by American Century Investments, cited by Christopher Browne in his *Little Book of Value Investing*, shows that had you stayed fully invested in the stock market (through an index fund, for example) from 1990 to 2005, a $10,000 investment would have grown to $51,354. But missing the ten best days over that period would have brought your take down to $31,994. If you'd missed the thirty biggest days (30 out of roughly 5400 days in the period), your investment would only have grown to $15,730.

So, in addition to the more fundamental reasons to set yourself up to be a long-term investor that we've covered earlier, there's the simple idea that you don't want to be out of the market when the good things are happening and the market is rewarding companies with upward price jumps.

There are at least a couple of good reasons, however, to pull ***some*** money out from time to time. One is to cover taxes generated by your investment gains from year to year. That's a perfectly legitimate use of your some of your winnings and usually does not make too big a dent in the corpus. If you can pay the taxes out of other sources of income and just let the investments grow untouched, great, but there is no shame in using this method. Another is when you have had a particularly good year and you would like to use some of your winnings to replenish your bond ladder or cash pad. Nothing wrong with that. There may also be certain temporary needs that come up. I would just counsel you to keep any amount you "borrow" from your account for temporary needs relatively small, or be sure you can replace it soon.

Question #3

Sometimes I stick with the <u>same old investments</u> because I just don't have time to look for something better. What should I do?

If you just happen to be invested in a way that is perfectly in keeping with the principles we've discussed throughout this book, then there is nothing wrong with "the same old investments." Good for you.

If you're not, you may be forgoing a lot of wealth growth and, depending on what your investments are, you may be vulnerable to a severe market downturn. Of course, if you don't have the proper safety net in place, a downturn could mean you will suffer dire consequences.

What should you do? Stop and dedicate the time required to getting set up correctly: Construct a proper safety net as described in Chapter 2 and locate a manager (or managers) who can invest your money in accordance with the principles of smart investing.

Question #4

Are there any "no brainer" investments I should definitely make?

Yes. Many companies with a 401K program offer contributions that match the amount an employee puts into the program each year. Right now you can put $15,500 a year into your 401K, or $20,500 if you are over age 50. For every dollar that your company will match that you contribute to the 401K, you have essentially made a 100% return on your investment immediately. This one's definitely a "no brainer." Even Warren Buffett couldn't get you a return like that. It's probably the best investment deal on the planet. Be sure that you contribute to your 401K plan ***at least*** the maximum amount that your company will match each year.

The other "no brainer" is investing through a Roth IRA. A regular IRA, just like your 401K, grows investments tax-deferred. But you have to pay tax when you take the money out. The Roth IRA, on the other hand, is not only tax deferred, it's free of tax even when you take it out, as long as you keep the money in the account until you're age 59 ½. And for certain reasons (to make a down payment on a first home, for example) you can take some money out before you are 59 ½ tax-free.

Question #5

What is the best thing I can do for my children – and perhaps grandchildren- to set them up for financial independence some day?

Good question. First, start contributing to a Roth IRA account for them beginning when they are about age twelve (or older). You can pay your children or grandchildren up to $4,000 per year for work they do for you and they can endorse that yearly paycheck right over to the investment entity that's set up to invest the Roth IRA funds for them. It is amazing what $4,000 per year starting at that age can grow to if invested wisely.

Second, when they are old enough, buy them a copy of this book and ask them to read it. Tell them you're going to give them a quiz and if they don't pass, you'll cut them out of the will. Just kidding, but what would you rather do: Give them a bunch of "fish" or teach them how to fish?

Giving them fish, in the investment context, is doing things like leaving them an inheritance in your will or leaving them a trust fund. If the amount you leave to them is so big that it is de-motivating, it could ruin their lives. If it is not that big, but they never learn how to "fish", they may well outlive the inheritance and "run out of fish." That's not a pleasant outcome either. The critical thing is helping them learn how to "fish", by becoming wise, confident investors on their own.

Question #6

What is the best use of the investment channels on TV, like CNBC and Bloomberg?

I'll describe this use to you very specifically. First, you find the remote control. Then you hit the "Off" button. I am dead serious.

I have seen more people do dumb things as a result of watching these channels than I care to recall. Why? Because dull TV does not get watched. It has to be fun and, most of all, ***exciting*** if it hopes to get watched and have ratings. So people get excited about what they hear and see on these channels. They get excited about a hot stock tip or about something bad happening at a company they own. It may be just a rumor, but it gets them worried and fearful. Getting excited is getting emotional, and emotion, in investing, can quickly overcome good logical thought.

Turn the TV off. Stay cool.

Question #7

What publications are helpful for people if they want to consider investing on their own?

There are two that are particularly good and are rooted solidly in the principles we've discussed in this book. As another plus, they are neither fun nor exciting, but they make very good sense and good reading if you have a natural interest in investing.

One is called Outstanding Investor's Digest (www.oid.com). It's an odd publication in that it does not come out on any regular schedule. When the publisher has enough good information to fill an issue (which can be either thirty two or sixty four pages in length), he sends an issue. You don't subscribe for a year, but for a certain number of issues. That way, when you get one, you can be sure it won't have filler. It's all good reading. I wish more publications did this.

The other is Morningstar StockInvestor (at www.morningstar.com, a monthly publication and on-line service. The team that publishes the StockInvestor for Morningstar does an excellent job and is steeped in the principles of value investing. They study about 1900 companies and provide meaningful analysis of each company and its prospects. They even have their own calculation of the company's fair value and their evaluation of how good a "moat" it has. Sometimes I agree with their fair value and "moat" calls and sometimes I do not, but they are clearly using the right principles in a rigorous way.

Question #8

Does it make sense to invest in insurance?

There are ways to "invest" through insurance (such as "whole life" policies), but I have never considered any of them attractive investments. I don't think of insurance as an investment —just as a cost of living. If you need a particular type of insurance, it needs to be in your budget and you should allow for it in your cash pad and safety net when figuring all your living expenses.

Specifically, if you have a home, you ***need*** home insurance. If you have a car you ***need*** car insurance. Likewise, if you have a body you need health insurance and long-term care insurance, though a lot of people sadly don't have the latter. If you have workers at your home (a gardener, for example) you may need workman's comp. If you have valuable art or jewelry, you would be well-advised to insure them. And if you have much net worth at all, you probably need a general liability umbrella policy.

The need for ***life*** insurance is relative to your personal situation. If you have plenty of money in your estate to leave for your loved ones, why do you need life insurance? If you need it, however, term life is usually reasonably priced.

Question #9

When I pick a fund, does the size of the market cap of companies they invest in matter?

"Market Cap," or market capitalization, is the number of outstanding shares times the share price at a given point in time. Large cap stocks are those with a valuation of over $5 billion, mid-caps are in the $5 billion to $1 billion range, small caps cover the $1 billion to $250 million range, and micro caps have valuations under $250 million.

As a class, small caps have generally outperformed the larger cap stocks over the long haul, but at any point in time, a great opportunity can be found in an undervalued company in ***any*** market cap: large, medium, small, or micro cap. Apart from the very small micro caps (under $150 million) – which I consider too risky for investment – I have found excellent opportunities and excellent returns in all the cap ranges.

Avoid a fund dedicated to only one cap class. A "multi-cap" fund is open to finding great opportunities wherever they exist, and that's what you want your manager to do, isn't it?

Question #10

What key factors should busy people look at to see if their portfolio growth is meeting their expectations?

A fund's short-term returns – i.e. what it has achieved in the last quarter or year-to-date versus the general market – may be interesting to look at, but are not meaningful and could lead you to an incorrect conclusion about the fund's potential. That's true if they are particularly good returns or particularly bad. They won't help you judge the investing acumen and "value added" brought by the fund's manager. The most dependable information is how well the manager has done versus the general market over the ***long*** term, and the longest term you can look at for any fund is "since inception." That's what to track first and foremost. If the manager has done a good job adding value, then his or her returns (after fees) should beat the S&P 500 by some percentage over the long haul, the bigger the better.

The other key factor is what happens to the fund's return when the going gets really tough. I only look at this at the end of a full year, so I am not being deluded by a quarterly "blip." If, after you've invested in a fund, the markets suffer a significant correction (down 10% or more), you'd like to see your fund be down less. This is a performance you can reasonably expect from the rigorous application of the value principles. Let's say a fund I was in fell as much as the market (or even more) during a bad year. I would give it another year to eighteen months to see if the manager is able to pull right back to overachieve the market and make up for the previous year's disappointment. Sometimes a manager buys shares knowing and expecting that the turnaround in a company's value won't come for two to three years. You don't want to overlook this possibility when you judge the situation.

Another indicator is the manager's quarterly letter. If you are only invested in one or two equity funds and perhaps one real estate partnership, it shouldn't be too taxing to read their complete letters quarterly. These should include full disclosure about what the fund owns and how its holdings are performing. These letters will tell you a lot about how good a job the manager is doing for you.

Question #11

I'm swamped with statements that come out monthly. Is it necessary to look at them that often? And what's the best way of keeping track of my overall portfolio, without having to spend too much time?

It's not necessary to look at monthly statements. A good ***quarterly*** review of what you own is best, and you want to look not just at the numbers, but really try to understand what the manager is doing and what he or she is thinking about the holdings. When you're in a long-term game, short term "over observation" is not healthy. You can even ignore everything except the "end-of-year" reports when it comes to evaluating ***performance***, and just read the quarterly letters to keep up with the interesting things happening with your holdings and enhance your feel for the manager's style and temperament.

Question #12

I've heard about people making a lot of money on IPO's and "Penny Stocks." Is there a place for those in my investment portfolio?

Penny stocks are shares selling for very low prices- typically under three dollars per share. Penny stocks are speculations, not investments. Sure, if you buy a $1 stock and it rises 1/8 in a day, you have a 12.5% gain. Wow! You always hear speculators boasting to their friends about how they got one of these and made some huge amount in a day or a week. They don't run up and tell their friends, though, when the stock falls 1/8, or 1/3. Penny stocks are extremely volatile, so that can easily happen. And wait until you see the commission you may pay to buy

20,000 shares of a $1 stock! Speculating is gambling. Wouldn't you have more fun in Las Vegas?

Generally, Initial Public Offerings (IPOs) would be considered speculative, too. After all, they are the first time a company is selling its stock to the public so there is no track record of the stock's performance yet. If the investor knows the industry and the company very well that is going public, though, an IPO may represent a very good opportunity. A case in point is the purchase of The Chicago Board of Trade when it went public, which we discussed earlier. I had owned The Chicago Mercantile Exchange for some time and had come to understand the economics of exchanges quite thoroughly. Before the Board of Trade ever went public, I had what I felt confident was a solid fair value calculated for it. The day the stock went public, the only question in my mind was whether it would be available at 50% (or less) of that fair value, or not. It did become available at that level, so I bought. Just buying an IPO because it's an IPO is a gambler's game. Buying when you know the company and the price is right it can make sense. This is something you (or your equity managers) will want to do only when very knowledgeable about the opportunity.

Who else could use a copy of this book?

When you consider your children, your business colleagues, and your friends and relatives, is there someone else in your life who could benefit from the information and approach outlined in this book? It could be the most valuable gift you ever give them.

Acknowledgements

There are a number of people to whom I owe a great debt of gratitude. They all helped in one way or another in making this book possible. First are my two business partners, Chris Doll, co-manager of the fund we run, and Terry Robinson, my partner in operating businesses for thirty years. Without their wisdom and support, I would never have been able to do this.

Many thanks to Rob Kuzmak, Mark Sellers, Jeff Herman, Flory and Frank Arcidiacono, Kelly Mattingly and Millie Town, and Chris Doll and C.T. Robinson for reviewing the text and giving me feedback and to The Hassells and the Hammertons and graphics designer Paige Thomas for their contributions to making the book's cover look so good. And thanks to the fine editing work of Barbara Ash and Debra DeSalvo.

Thanks to Rich Reis for his suggestion to include questions from "busy people" about investing. Also special thanks to Buck Blessing, Bruce Shepard, and Stuart Scott for their insights on real estate investing and particularly to Buck for working with me to develop the system for vetting private real estate managers and their deals.

Also thank you to Melanie Tutt for her excellent photographic work.

Recommended Reading

If you are interested in reading more about some of the aspects of investing discussed in this book, here are a few well-written books that deal intelligently with their subject, listed by subject:

On Equity Investing Strategies

Fisher, Philip A., *Common Stocks and Uncommon Profits*, New York: John Wiley & Sons, Inc., 1958.

Glassman, James K., *The Secret Code of the Superior Investor*, New York: Crown Business, Division of Random House, Inc, 2002.

Graham, Benjamin, *The Intelligent Investor*. New York: Harper & Row Publishers, 1973.

Hagstrom, Robert G., *The Warren Buffett Way*, New York: John Wiley & Sons, Inc., 1995.

On Real Estate Investing Strategies

McLean, Andrew and Eldred, Gary W., PhD, *Investing in Real Estate*, New York: John Wiley & Sons, Inc., 2006

On Behavioral Economics as it Can Affect Investing

Belsky, Gary and Gilovich, Thomas, *Why Smart People Make Big Money Mistakes*, New York: Fireside, Division of Simon & Schuster, 1999

On The Wisdom of the Focused Portfolio

Hagstrom, Robert G., *The Warren Buffett Portfolio*, New York: John Wiley & Sons, Inc., 1999.

Index